John,   1-7-94

With all best wishes
and many happy returns
from all of us at 'the Haven'.

Jan + Brenda
xx

THE BOOK OF MAIDENHEAD

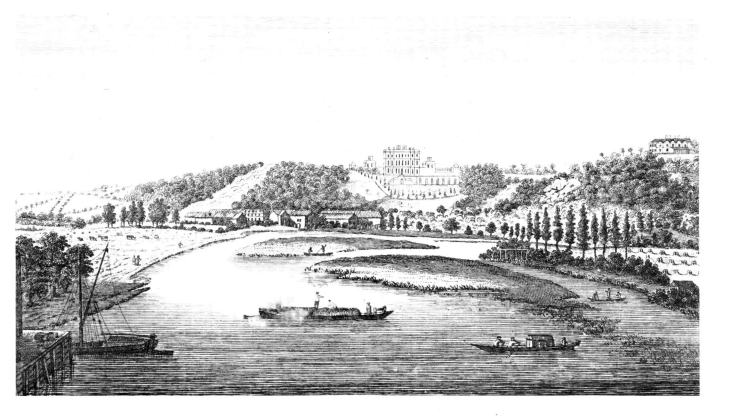

FRONT COVER: Cliveden from Maidenhead Bridge
in the 18th century.

BACK: Borough Coat of Arms.

The female race of 1819 at Maidenhead.

THE BOOK OF MAIDENHEAD

THE STORY OF THE TOWN

BY

TOM MIDDLETON

BARRACUDA BOOKS LIMITED
CHESHAM, BUCKINGHAMSHIRE, ENGLAND
MCMLXXV

FIRST PUBLISHED BY BARRACUDA BOOKS LIMITED
BUCKINGHAM, ENGLAND in 1975
SECOND IMPRESSION 1977
SECOND EDITION 1983
THIRD EDITION 1988

PRINTED AND BOUND BY
WOOLNOUGH BOOKBINDING
WELLINGBOROUGH, ENGLAND

JACKET PRINTED BY
CHENEY AND SONS LIMITED
BANBURY, OXON

PHOTO LITHOGRAPHY BY
SOUTH MIDLANDS LITHO PLATES LIMITED
LUTON, ENGLAND

ADDITIONAL MATERIAL TYPESET BY
KEY COMPOSITION
NORTHAMPTON, ENGLAND

© TOM MIDDLETON 1975

THIRD EDITION 1988

ISBN 0 86023 429 0

Contents

HRH The Prince of Wales 8

Foreword by John Smith 8

Preface by Stanley Platt 9

Acknowledgements 9

Sing of the Road.. 10

Introduction: A Place to Remember 11

The Gateway 12

Mind your Manors 21

1688 and all That 29

They Built Jerusalem 32

To the Thames—a Son 39

War Haven 58

Down by the Riverside 62

Among those Present 77

High Street Story 89

All That Jazz 110

To Shape a Town 124

Current Affairs 138

A Change of Programme 144

Bibliography 146

Index 146

Foreword

by the first High Steward of the Royal Borough of Windsor and Maidenhead,
HRH Prince Charles, The Prince of Wales

I recommend this book to any Maidonian who wishes to find out about the origins of his town and the history of his ancestors. It is packed with every conceivable item of information and has obviously caused the author an immense amount of hard work and research.

One thing is certain and that is that this book will be of invaluable assistance to the new and inexperienced High Steward of the Borough of Windsor *and* Maidenhead . . .

BUCKINGHAM PALACE.
May 1975.

Foreword

by the last High Steward of Maidenhead

Every town is the better, and a pleasanter place to live in, if it has a clear identity of its own —if its people know about their town and are fond of it, warts and all. Maidenhead is indeed an old and honourable place, with plenty of history and a special personality, but nowadays its population grows and changes more rapidly than ever before. Therefore a book like this is worth a lot, to engage the newcomer and to remind the rest of us.

Moreover, who better to write it than Tom Middleton, editor of our newspaper and chronicler of our doings—and of our misdoings, if he can get to hear of them. His amused and kindly eye is perfectly suited to this riverside town, which has never disregarded pleasure. By writing this book and so giving us a consciousness of time and place, he does this town and us yet one more service.

SHOTTESBROOKE,
MAIDENHEAD.
April 1975.

8

Preface

by the former Clerk to the Borough Council

It was in 1909, after more than 300 years of existence as a town that the first and only comprehensive history of Maidenhead was published. The author, John Wesley Walker, records with truth in his Preface that 'if Maidenhead has not been especially rich in history it has been still less rich in historians'.

More information is now available about our past, particularly our earliest ancestors and The Book of Maidenhead has been able to make use of this and to bring the town's history up to date in other ways.

The major changes and rapid growth during the past 75 years which outstrip those which took place during the previous 300 years have dictated the necessity of publishing a new history of Maidenhead to cover this period. No one is better qualified to do this than Tom Middleton. Since he joined the editorial staff of the Maidenhead Advertiser nearly 30 years ago he has taken a deep interest in searching out and recording on a broad canvas the facts about the town's life and development. He writes with warmth and sympathy but is nevertheless meticulous about the accuracy of his work.

The publisher is to be congratulated on using photography so well in this History. The excellent photographic records combined with the interesting and informative narrative make this work a worthy complement to Walker's History of Maidenhead.

HOLCOMBE, HARVEST HILL
MAIDENHEAD

Acknowledgements

I am indebted to many people who have volunteered offers of help with pictures and family documents. My special thanks go to Mrs Margaret Pitcher, Mr Tom Stuchbery, Mr John Brooks, and Mr Johnnie Walker, who provided rare pictures and documents; Mr John Brown, Mr Ray Weng of Maidenhead and District Archaeological and Historical Society, Mr Eric Brooks, and Mr Sidney Horsham who have kindly read manuscripts; Mr James Powell, district librarian, his deputy Mr Barry Lawrence, and Miss Pat Thomas of the reference library, for their invaluable help with original material, advice, information and the essential reservation facility; Mr John Neal who provided pictures; Lady Liddell, Mr Tony Pickford who re-drew Alderman Silver's map, Mr Gerald Baylis, Mr Alan Davidson, Advertiser chief photographer, Berkshire County Record Office, Mr Leslie Cram of Reading Museum, and past generations of Advertiser reporters.

Finally, extra special thanks to my wife who took over the mowing of lawns, dug the vegetable garden and kept a stream of coffee going for late night sessions. The index is largely her work. I only typed it.

Sing of the Road

To come to rest beside the Great West Road,
Among the dusty bustle of the street of inns,
Was peace upon a route where Wessex Men
Fought for England. There, Mounted Micks
Made ribald fellows in the passing show,
As ostlers and stable boys made haste
Among the hurried wheels and hooves
That rang the cobbled way.

The huddled inns, by lantern's light
Engulfed the throng, and trapped
Their stories of the road. Crescendoes
From the tavern bars gushed through the night
For only watchmen on their rounds to hear.
The morning took them all away.
Time rides down the road as well as man—
Untrapped by clocks.

The road alone has time, the people
Clustered to this friendly thing;
Building their homes, neighbours all.
An artery man's tried to twist, to plan,
Will bear no tourniquet to stem its life;
The Great road has us all,
To lock us in or make us free—
The town's biography.

Dedication

for Elsie

A Place to Remember

Ever since crossing Maidenhead Thicket in a mail coach was risking a hold-up by highwaymen, Maidenhead has been a place to remember. There are all sorts of reasons for this. It was the terminus for the first stretch of Brunel's Great Western Railway. It was a Thamesside resort where a good time could be had by all who could afford it, and the Brigade of Guards Boat Club gave it a social standing to which it was probably not entitled. Its visitors' list, if you included the two big houses of Taplow Court and Cliveden entitled it to a special Maidenhead section in Debrett.

Many people hold to the view that nothing happened here before the Victorians came. In fact, it was in the mainstream of English history from the moment that the first invaders came up the Thames. The men of Wessex, of which Maidenhead was a part, created England.

Its literary tradition can be traced to the 17th century, its farms to the first men to plant seed, and its first inhabitants to the Early Stone Age. There are quite beautiful examples of the flint knappers' art, and Maidenhead has been one of the richest places in England for the study of early man.

Great historical figures have been connected with the town, from Sir Walter Raleigh who was tried here, to Winston Churchill who was thrown in the Thames. Its business life was organised and developed by the Victorians with remarkable foresight and enterprise, and until the population explosion in the 1950s it had remained largely undisturbed, being one of the last of the towns close to the booming South East to feel the effects of the Development Age.

The violent upheavals that have taken place within it are subsiding and there are plenty of signs that Maidenhead has adjusted to the new age, and that its essential character and the people in it who give it its personality are not much different from those who gave it a touch of fun and adventure in Victorian and Edwardian Days.

There are signs also that the present is much better than we give it credit for, that many of our troubles have been overcome and that the lot of many Maidonians of Victorian days will not bear comparison with the social advances that have been made.

Stone Age man left his hand axe at Furze Platt—
c 250,000 years ago.

12

The Gateway

Stone Age man was here. He left his memoranda at Furze Platt. His axes and tools were all over the place, making Maidenhead one of the richest spots for research into this period in the Thames Valley. From Courtlands in Shoppenhangers Road to New Road, Bourne End, travelling through Cookham and Cookham Rise, these first people went about their business of hunting and toolmaking. At Cannon Court Farm, Furze Platt there appears to have been a considerable flint knapping industry. It is one of the richest palaeolithic sites in Britain. Some 589 hand axes and tools have been found there. In 1919 the largest known palaeolithic hand axe in Britain, and probably in Europe, was picked up at Furze Platt. It is 12⅝th ins. long.

Boyn Hill, Linden Avenue, Courthouse Road, Belmont Park Avenue, Spencers Road, Cromwell Road, and All Saints Avenue had prehistoric occupation. Stone Age man was busy all along the curve of the Thames, from Cookham to Maidenhead, over which route so much history was to flow. That curve, incidentally, came about when a glacier moved south westwards into the valley of the Thames to dam the river at Bourne End, causing it to flow southwards to Maidenhead. This was our beginning.

Because man needed to live near water, the Thames Valley was one of the first places where the human voice was heard. It was in the Thames Valley that the remains of our first ancestor were found—Swanscombe woman.

More than 10,000 years ago the rhinoceros, elephant, horse, and musk ox were fairly commonplace. The skull of a musk ox, to provide the first proof that it had existed in Britain, was found near the Dumb Bell at Taplow, together with the remains of a mammoth (elephant), a rhinoceros, and a horse, in 1855. There is also evidence that perma frost reached Taplow.

A wide range of implements from the Middle Stone Age were left at Bray and Braywick, notably at Moor Farm, Holyport. Much may still lie buried by the centuries along this first pathway of man, scattered near the tribal tracks that were to lead into the history of England.

About 2,000 BC the New Stone Age farmers came along. (Swanscombe Woman was dated about 250,000 BC.) They were followed up the Thames by the Celts, Romans, Saxons, and Danes, before England became a kingdom. Berkshire men helped to bring this about. Saxon chiefs in the Maidenhead area, if not actually participating in the victory, had every reason to support it, giving Maidenhead a direct link with the foundation of the Kingdom of England, which was brought about by King Alfred of Wantage.

These New Stone Age farmers were the first people to plant seed. They began a crude field system here, and because of this they stayed to harvest their crops. Thus began the permanent settlements, and the art of the potter. Pots were needed for storage as well as daily use. There were neolithic families at Canon Hill. This new way of life which brought possessions, also brought greed and eventually war. Maidenhead was to be brushed by the men of battle. For men moving into the conflict, Maidenhead, then as now, was the Gateway to the Upper Thames.

Beyond Maidenhead the river was shallow and marshy. Also, many days' march away was the fertile land of the rolling Berkshire Downs. Across the top of the Downs ran the Ridgeway—part of the Icknield Way—one of the first main roads of England. The Ridgeway and the river were a trade route to Europe all the way from Wiltshire. From Wiltshire an old trackway linked the route with Devon. Gold ornaments found in a Saxon chief's grave at Taplow, believed to be Taeppa or Aella, head of the Bretwalda, were probably carried along this route from Wales where the Celts had primitive gold mines.

When the Celts invaded the South they also came through the Gateway to the Upper Thames. They were from the powerful Belgic race who crossed to England in the last century BC, dropping quite a lot of iron swords and tools into the Thames in passing through Maidenhead. The Celts began to change our culture. An improved field system emerged where grain for Roman legions was to be grown. Among the places where they settled were Cox Green and Knowl Hill. The Belgic tribe inhabiting Windsor Forest, (which spilt into Maidenhead) is thought to have been the Bibroci, a clan of the Attrebates whose woodland home was Calleva Atrebatus (Silchester). A block of local authority flats obscures a farm which began in neolithic times. Certainly the first farmers there lived in primitive huts. The kilns at Altwood Bailey, where the potters made domestic utensils and roof tiles could have been part of a farm or manor involving this early settlement. On the Thicket is the Belgic fort—Robin Hood's Arbour—which later became a Roman outpost for a sizeable camp spreading to Tittle Row.

The Romans also left their signatures in the Maidenhead area. They got along well with the Celts and did not interfere in local government. The principal battle of their campaign was at Wallingford and they pushed on to set up one of their ten principal towns at Silchester. They divided the land into large sections for tax collection by local chiefs, housing them in villas, which were cottage farmsteads. There were villas at Castle Hill, Cox Green, Feen's Farm, Littlewick, and Canhurst Farm, Waltham St Lawrence. Taxes were paid in corn. The Castle Hill villa was discovered by Alderman Richard Silver when he was planting trees. His family is still here. The only thing we know about the Castle Hill chief is that he took the occasional hot bath at Etruria. His bath and hot water system survived him. Until recently, the Roman road could be traced from Braywick, parallel with the Braywick Road, across High Street, and Kidwells Park. The Romans also built a radial road system from Silchester. One of these went through Reading, Twyford, Waltham St Lawrence, Braywick, and Bray. The Camlet Way from St Albans came through Maidenhead on its way to Silchester, passing over Castle Hill. It is thought that soldiers from the Thicket Camp provided patrols for this civilian route. Oysters, which were a choice food among well-off Romans, were eaten in large numbers at White Waltham. They left the shells as evidence.

Three hundred years of Roman rule civilised the ancient Britons and an agricultural economy was established. In the early part of the 5th century the Romans left. The Saxon invasion began about AD 450. The Saxon wars raged for 300 years. The Saxons set up seven kingdoms, among them the West Saxons of Wessex. The story of Maidenhead is concerned with these men of Wessex. Their stronghold was in the Wantage area. The defences of

Wessex stretched along the south of the Thames. Control of this southern territory was vital to them against the King of Mercia.

The Danes first appeared round the coast in AD 832. Eventually they set off on the same historic route arriving at the Gateway to the Upper Thames. They were heading deep into Wessex and were to make Reading their stronghold. There is a case for believing that they disembarked at Maidenhead from their longboats and fought their way to Reading overland. This is supported by the view that their longboats would have been too heavy to have been dragged over the shallows and marshy sections upstream; also that their battles were fought at Kennet crossings. Whatever the truth, local place names which crop up all over the place such as at Danes Ditches, Hurley, at least commemorate their passing. But the men of Wessex were to defeat the Danes when Alfred led them to victory at the Battle of Ashdown to establish the kingdom of England. The retreat, like the advance would have been through the Gateway, putting Maidenhead into the jetstream of history.

These ancient people established much upon which we have built. We did not surrender the fields of the Neolithic farmers until the 1960s. Our counties and hundreds and the manorial system stem from the 10th century, and the English church is linked with the first missionaries, one of whom was St Birinus who is said to have baptised the first local christians at Bapsey Pond, Taplow.

But the 1066 land storm by the Normans was total and impoverishing to the point of starvation. King William ordered Domesday to record the value of his seized possessions after the pillage had begun. Domesday says of Maidenhead, then called South Ellington: 'It was worth 60s, now 40s'. This represented a one-third fall in value from Edward the Confessor's England. But the name of one man who came over with the Normans has passed into the history of Maidenhead, although we have changed the spelling—Pinkney.

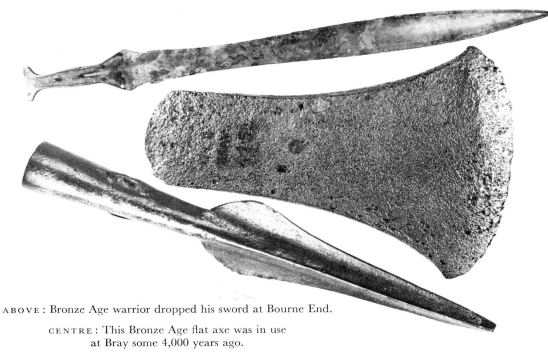

ABOVE : Bronze Age warrior dropped his sword at Bourne End.

CENTRE : This Bronze Age flat axe was in use
at Bray some 4,000 years ago.

BELOW : Maidenhead's military focus was the river: this socketed spear-
head from the same period was found under the Sounding Arch.
(Thames Conservancy Collection).

LEFT: A Romanised native used this chopper at Bray.
(Thames Conservancy Collection).

CENTRE: This Iron Age settlement at Robin Hood's Arbour, Maidenhead
Thicket, was taken over by the Romans.

RIGHT: One of 12 iron currency bars, once used by Maidonians some
2000 years ago. (Reading Museum).

ABOVE: Tazza Bowl, *c* AD20, found at Knowl Hill. It would have been used for anointing oil. (Maidenhead and District Archaeological and Historical Society: Reitlinger Museum).

BELOW: Bapsey Pond, where the first local Christians were said to have been baptised around AD600.

LEFT: St Birinus and the first baptisms of Maidenhead.
Stained glass window at Taplow Church.

RIGHT: Drinking horn buried with the Saxon Taeppa at Taplow.

BELOW: Gold buckles—part of Taeppa's worldly goods.

ABOVE: Taplow Mound, where Taeppa was laid
to rest in the 6th century.

BELOW: Another of Taeppa's trinkets.

19

The Taplow Bowl—from Taeppa's burial chamber. (Courtesy British Museum).

Mind your Manors

South Ellington, the Domesday name for Maidenhead, did not survive for obvious reasons. South Ellington, variously spelt in old documents, could have been no more than a cluster of dwellings, if that. It was probably so called to distinguish it from the North Town area, where a medieaval longhouse dominated the Manor of Spencer or Knight Ellington. Early settlers wisely chose the higher ground above flood level. South Ellington could have been a much younger place. The busiest part of the district from early times, and the place which had the most metropolitian air, was the riverside. The river led to the sea and Europe, a highway for trade as well as invasion. There was a hythe (wharf) there. The Great Hill of Taplow, where Taplow Court and Cliveden stand, was christened Mai Dun by the Celts. Saxons probably spoke of their hythe as the Mai Dun Hythe. The old name for the crossing by the wharf—Maidunhythe—came to be preferred to South Ellington, although at one time both names were in use.

Although Maidenhead was 200 years away from shaping up as a small township when the Normans got here, there was an estate plan which enclosed most of the area that we know today as Maidenhead. The division into Saxon hundreds—collections of 100 homes—saw to that. The Hundred of Bray was Bray parish only. Beynhurst consisted of Bisham, Hurley, Remenham, White Waltham, and Shottesbrooke. In the Hundred of Cookham were Cookham itself, Binfield, and Sunninghill. Waltham St Lawrence was in the Hundred of Wargrave. Within the hundreds were a number of manors—administrative units, not homes—held by distinguished people. In Saxon times, Cookham and Bray were both royal manors and remained so under the Normans and Plantagenets. Cookham was bequeathed to the crown about 975 by Ealdorman Aelfheah, and remained royal until 1818.

Sub-divisions of the manors came when gifts of land were made to royal favourites. The king, church, and barons ruled in Norman times. Their occupation was disastrous for Saxon lord, smallholder, and everyone else. They stripped the country to its last grain of corn, and Maidenhead was corn-growing country. The ring of small Saxon manors round Maidenhead was run by a few men who were to be punished for their patriotism to Edward the Confessor's England. Rheinbold the Priest, with interests in Cookham and Bray, was a lucky one. He had been the Confessor's chancellor. The Conqueror, wary of priests, left him unharmed. But Esgar the Staller—an office equivalent to Master of the Horse today—lord of the manor of Hurley, was stripped of his estates. Bondi, saxon lord of Bisham, suffered the same fate, as did Asgot of Taplow. Another loyal lord was Aldrea of Dorney. He was a friend of Morkar, Earl of the Northumbrians who fought with Hereward the Wake in the Saxons' last stand at Ely.

One manor that did not change hands was Shottesbrooke, and for an intriguing reason. It was held by Edward the Confessor's Queen Edith, with the manors of Remenham,

21

Waltham St Lawrence, and Warfield. The Queen's tenant was the father of Alward the Goldsmith. Goldsmiths were also money lenders. He was an allodial tenant, meaning that he paid no rent. One theory is that he or his son gave financial aid to influential people. Even kings and queens needed money. The Conqueror continued the arrangement. In fact the manor was held as an extraordinary form of grand serjeantry—the right and duty of refashioning the crown at each coronation, which Alward was presumably qualified to do.

Shottesbrooke came to embrace the greater part of White Waltham in the Manor of Berry, which has come down from Saxon times practically intact to the present Lord of the Manor of Berry, John Smith, last High Steward of the Borough of Maidenhead. At one time Berry belonged to the Benedictine Abbey at Chertsey. The adjoining Manor of Heywood—the name continues in Heywood Park—was once part of the heritage of King Harold. He gave it to Waltham Abbey, Essex. Curiously, one of the earliest recorded uses of the name 'Maidenhuth' was in 1273, some seven years before Maidenhead Bridge was built, by Reginald de Maidenhuth, Canon of the Holy Cross of Waltham Abbey. That he was 'of Maidenhuth' and not 'of Heywood' or 'of South Ellington' suggests that he chose the better known place.

William gave Taplow to the hated Odo Bishop of Bayeux, one of the leaders of the rape of England. Hurley went to Geoffrey de Mandeville, Bisham to Henry de Ferriers, and Dorney to Miles Crispin. So was Maidenhead Normalised.

A new name on the Cookham side arrived with the Normans—Ghilo de Pinkney, high in favour with the Conqueror, judging from the massive grants of land. At Domesday he was at the Manor of Ellington. The name derives from Picquigny on the Somme. By the 15th century it had become the Manor of Pinkneys and a Pinkney remained there for almost 400 years. The family became linked by marriage with the Hobys of Bisham. The manor briefly belonged to Sir John Norreys about 1415, at about the time that he began to build Ockwells, but his widow sold it.

Two smaller manors in Bray which appear to have started with royal patronage were Cresswells and Ockwells. Hugh de St Philibert was given Cresswells. He 'brought the measures of wine to the morning meal of the lord king'. Another favoured servant was Ricardo de Norreys, the Queen's cook. In 1268 Henry III rented him a piece of Windsor Forest for 40s a year, called Ochold. Sir John Norreys, master of the wardrobe to Henry VI rebuilt the house as the Ockwells Manor we know today. He died in 1416.

The Manor of Ive, which stretched along the Bray-Cookham boundary, from which we get St Ives Road, was once owned by John Ive. He was there in 1297. No. 11 High Street, on the corner of St Ives Road, was the site of the Bulle Inn. It was converted into a chapel by William Wilberforce, brother of Bishop Wilberforce of Oxford, who came to live at Ives Place. He regrettably added the prefix 'Saint'. Ive Manor was part of the estates of the Priory of Austin Canons at Bisham. Robert de Ferriers gave the Manor of Bustleham, Bisham, to the Knights Templars who made it their home from 1312 to 1335. When Henry VIII dissolved the monasteries, the priory was discontinued and the king immediately founded a Benedictine Abbey there which lasted only seven months. He then gave Bisham to his fourth wife, Ann of Cleaves, who thus came to have both Bisham and Ives.

Ives became part of the fabric of Maidenhead. The Town Hall and the Library stand on it. It came down through Richard Whitfield to the Powney family. In 1786, Penyston Portlock Powney of Grovebury and Ives Place bought Ockwells Manor. He had succeeded his father as Verderer (superintendent of trees) of Windsor Forest. The Victorians named three roads after him. He became High Steward of Maidenhead in 1764.

Two great figures of history are connected with Bisham. Warwick the Kingmaker is buried there and Elizabeth was imprisoned there by her sister Mary before she became Elizabeth I. Her keeper was Sir Thomas Hoby.

Hurley, after Geoffrey de Mandeville, became a Benedictine Priory, but Henry VIII transferred the manor to the crown. He gave it to Charles Howard, who sold it to Leonard Chamberleyn in 1543. In 1545 Chamberleyn sold it to John Lovelace. The receipt was handed to Lovelace at the font of St Paul's, a usual place to meet for business in those days.

Shottesbrooke, which remained undisturbed through the general post of manors and the various land deals, had a church when Domesday Book was compiled. It was also to become closely involved in the history of Maidenhead. Fragments of the Norman building were still there at the turn of the century. In 1337 the manor passed to Sir William Tressell who endowed a college there. It was one of the smallest of its kind and known as the College of St John the Baptist, with a warden and five priests. It is thought that the fine brass of a priest and layman in the church represent the first warden of the college and his brother.

There is another monument of a later warden, William Throckmorton, of whom a miniature stone effigy dressed in doctor's robes lies in a stone coffin. These colleges took no monastic vows. Sir William rebuilt the church to the south of the college and connected the college to it with a covered way. A blocked-up arch in the south transcept shows where the passage entered the church. There is also a brass of Richard Gyll, a servant in the household of Henry VII.

By the 17th century Francis Cherry became squire of Shottesbrooke, a pious and learned Jacobite who refused the oath of allegiance to William and Mary. The revolt that brought them to the throne was plotted at Ladye Place, Hurley.

Little is known of the origins of Shoppenhangers Manor beyond the fact that the name means 'hanging woods'. Its farms used to reach Braywick and the oldest buildings were pulled down when the place was turned into an hotel. It was rebuilt in the style of a rich merchant's home of the 17th century by Thornton Smith between the wars as an experiment in elegant living. He used a team of Norfolk craftsmen. It was built of period material which he had collected, such as stained glass from Selby Abbey, the linenfold panelling in the dining room, and was furnished with treasures. Thornton Smith was a connoisseur and probably the best known furniture restorer in Europe. When he died the contents and house were sold.

The Manor of Bray eventually passed to the Grenfell family. Pascoe bought the manor from the Crown in 1818. He bought Ives (1800) and Shoppenhangers (1801). His son Charles Pascoe bought Ockwells and Kimbers (1846), Taplow Court from Lord Orkney and Lowbrooks, adjoining Ockwells (1852). He then added Cresswells (1860), Philberts (1863), Foxleys (1864), and many smallholdings. They passed to Pascoe Grenfell's great-grandson who was created Baron Desborough in 1905. He died in 1945, one of the most brilliant men of his age, at 89. The estate was dissolved in 1953.

[Medieval Latin Domesday manuscript text — two entries in original handwriting]

ABOVE: Domesday entry for Cookham.
BELOW: And for Bray.

ABOVE: Ye Olde Bell, Hurley—12th century inn.
BELOW: Bisham Abbey.

24

ABOVE LEFT: Priest and layman in brass at
Shottesbrooke: 14th century.
ABOVE RIGHT: Bricked up arch, once the way to St John's College,
endowed 1377 by Sir William Trissell.
BELOW: Domesday entry for Shottesbrooke.

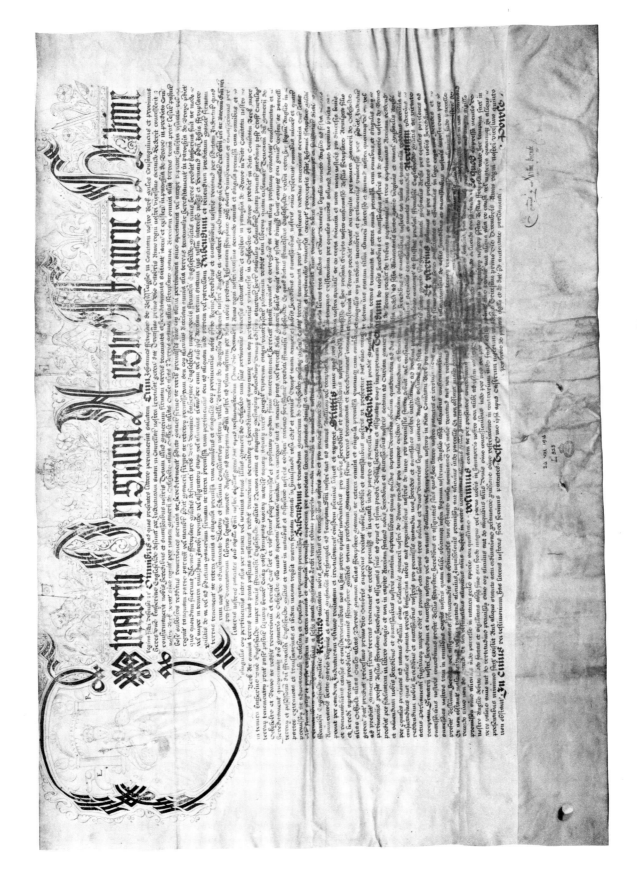

Royal grant of the Manor of Ockeholte (Ockwells): 16th century.
(Victoria & Albert Museum).

1605 Hoby family memorials at Bisham Church.

27

ABOVE: Shoppenhangers Manor.
BELOW: The man who moulded it: Thornton Smith.

28

1688 and all That

As the men of Maidenhead were linked with the men of Wessex who set up the kingdom of England, so were they part of the peace which followed the revolution of 1688, again helping to change the course of history in England. Great historical figures and thousands of armed men crossed the river to Maidenhead by its militarily important bridge. Saturday morning shoppers who crowd the narrow High Street walk, do so in the wake of great historical events. If the majority of them were to turn out in 17th century costume and if everyone who owns a horse rode it into the street equipped as cavalier, roundhead, Irish Dragoon or Scots Guard, the smell of horses and leather, the jangle of the implements of war and the noise of the throng would not match the gatherings of fighting men which have taken place in that place.

During the Civil War, the Earl of Manchester's Troop was quartered in Maidenhead. Charles I's outpost was at Reading. Troop movement in the area was considerable. The Parliamentarians came here in thousands to muster a brigade on the Thicket. There were 16,000 foot and 3,000 cavalry assembled for an assault on Reading. After the Battle of Aldermaston Lane, the Earl of Leicester, general commanding the Parliamentary forces, returned with his troops through Maidenhead.

Charles I also had a personal relationship with the town. It was at the old Greyhound Inn, now National Westminster Bank North, that he met two of his children on July 15, 1647. Crowds lined the street with green boughs and flowers. They had come to see the little Princess Elizabeth and the Duke of Gloucester. Afterwards they went to Caversham with their father. Cromwell was supposed to have seen the meeting. The Rushworth Records recall that Cromwell said that he had lately seen the tenderest sight ever his eyes had beheld.

It was probably to the old Greyhound that Sir Walter Raleigh was brought to be tried for conspiracy against James I in 1603. The judges met in Maidenhead, presumably because of the risk of infection from the Black Death in London. On this occasion he was found not guilty.

The most significant military confrontation to take place locally, which did affect the course of history, occurred during the revolution of 1688. The revolt came about because nobles and statesmen decided to get rid of James II, a Roman Catholic, and to replace him with the Prince of Orange, protestant husband of James II's daughter Mary. One of the leaders of the revolt was Lord Lovelace of Ladye Place, Hurley, where the plot was hatched. Others included the Earls of Devonshire, Danby, Shrewsbury, Lumley, Compton, Russell, and Sidney.

They met in a cellar, access to which was gained through a door under the stairs. On the door was carved a rose. Because of this, the plotters invented a phrase which has passed into the language. When going down to the cellar they said they were going 'sub rosa'.

Lovelace was captured early in the conflict, but in the closing stages the action moved to Maidenhead. The Prince's men were advancing towards London when they were involved in a skirmish at Twyford with the King's Irish Dragoons, (known as 'The Mounted Micks' through long service in Ireland). The dragoons withdrew to Maidenhead with the intention of making a stand at the Bridge. Also in Maidenhead, on this 10th day of December, 1688, were two battalions of the Scots Guards under Lt-Gen. Douglas. Samuel Pepys recorded their presence. Some historians claim that Maidenhead people frightened the 'Micks' away by 'beating a Dutch retreat in the night'. It seems a most unlikely story. I favour the account given in the Portledge Papers. These are a collection of letters written to Richard Coffin of Portledge, Bideford, by Richard Lampthorn, published in 1928. If Pepys was right in the location of Douglas's troops on the 10th, the defeat of James II was at Maidenhead where the Prince's army met the dragoons and General Douglas's troops. Of the engagement between the Irish Dragoons and the Prince's men, Lampthorn wrote, 'They fought smartly and it is said that a party of the Lord Douglas stood by and looked on without fighting so that the Irish were fain to fly being many of them killed and an abundance wounded'. Soldiers became dispirited and several commanders began to declare for the Prince of Orange. 'They disarmed and turned out such as were Roman Catholics out of their companies'.

As a result of this engagement the Prince of Orange was invited to London. The man selected by the citizens to meet him was Sir Robert Clayton. The Clayton and the East families became linked in marriage and lived at Hall Place, Burchetts Green, where the family connection with the revolution is commemorated in relief plaster work. Hall Place is now the Berkshire College of Agriculture.

Thus a revolution which began at Hurley ended at Maidenhead to begin the reign of William and Mary.

ABOVE: Braywick House, c 1675. The Adam brothers designed a new west wing a century later, for Lord Coleraine. The legend has it that the White Lady emerges from a tunnel and passes through a first floor window! Today's occupants are Pandair, of the P&O Group.

Frescoes at Hall Place, of William and Mary—commemorating the Clayton-East connection with the 1688 revolution.

ABOVE: Shottesbrooke Park.

BELOW: Ladye Place, Hurley.

Sir Robert Clayton. (The Mansell Collection).

31

LETTER V.

YE, who the Gospel to your views expound,
By fools thought learned, and by few thought sound;
Who charity, and social bonds despise—
Hell's in your hearts! and Sion in your eyes!
Whose saintly looks and sable vestments hide
The filth and nastiness conceal'd inside.
In vain ye rave; so frantic in your spite—
I'll drag your works of darkness into light;
And brandish o'er your backs th' AVENGING ROD,
Who, fed by Mammon, teach the flock of GOD!!!
Explaining as ye list the Heavenly Book,
Till SION's SHEPHERD turns to *Satan's Cook*;
And feeds his flock with Gospel till they're fit,
And serves up SION's SHEEP at *Satan's spit.*

Holy Minister,

  MY motto in this Letter I apply to Methodism in general, and not to your Reverence, who, for all that I know to the contrary, may be an exception to the general rule, and in no wise deserving the harsh reflections these few rhymes are meant to deal out amongst the Puritans. I make this apology to you at starting, that you may read the remainder of this Letter with greater self-complacency, and, consequently, in a better frame of mind.

  I hope, most worthy Sir, you have paid attention to the hints I gave you in my last, about *certain Missses* parading the streets in fancy dresses, and light airy garbs; setting all rules of sobriety at defiance—inasmuch that the people might well exclaim, " Can these be the daughters of *Baal*, our *High Priest?* I hope, in your discourse on the Sabbath, you will endeavour, by your preaching, to strip those Ladies of this summer cloathing; and as the winter is coming on fast, put something more decent on their backs, which will be better both for the minds and bodies.

A want of decency's a want of sense— Immodest dress admits of no defence:

And as you have succeeded in banishing the Play Actors, I have not the least doubt but that you will succeed likewise in persuading these young Damsels to array themselves with more propriety; for I have been told that they form *part* of your Congregation. I will now leave the young Ladies to themselves; hoping, however, to see no more of their green gauze dresses, which scarcely covered them better than *Eve's fig-leaves*—and they have not our first Parents excuse for such simple apparel, as the young Ladies may recollect that there were *no Mantua-makers in Paradise,* as you, most worthy Divine, may have informed them.

  I am told, most intelligent Explainer of Christian doubts, that the Methodists, with your *Holiness* at their head, have offered *Rewards* for the detection of the Authors of certain Papers which have been handed about to the prejudice of their characters—(that is, to the explosion of their Magazine of Hypocrisy.) Now this is *just as it ought to be*, and shews that the *Gentlemen* are stung—for the saddle always pinches the tender place. As to your *Rewards*, the very idea is a complete *Humbug!* Who, in the name of Truth, would ever believe for one moment, that a set of Ragged Fellows from a Conventicle would think of *paying* FIFTY POUNDS! As much would I expect to see Fifty Pounds collected in *halfpence* in your *money-dish,* for a Charity Sermon. No! No! You have done very well by offering a *Reward*; but as to *paying* any body Fifty Pounds, no one can *Swallow* that, I am certain, without your Worship can; but I would much rather see you pocket the affront.

  I understand, most saintly Apostle of the New Doctrine, that you have satisfied your mind in regard to your reception in the next world—that you are already registered on the muster-roll of Heaven. When I tell you I understand all this, I mean to say *that you have* asserted this fact from your pulpit. I do not mean, most worthy Divine, to contradict your assertion; but I intend to declare, that such an assertion amounts to the *blackest blasphemy*; and I say likewise, that the man who could have the impiety to make such a declaration, under the mask of teaching Christianity, is more dangerous to the community at large, than any band of Strollers acting obscene and immoral Plays; and ought to be banished, like them, from all Society. But, oh! Man of high Reputation! I can scarcely believe it possible that you could have been ignorant enough to frame such fictions, or wicked enough to promulgate such ideas! Your flock of *Scape Goats*, oh! worthy Man! must have belied you; and have only listened to your discourses to take away your character. Beware then, in future, of the *Methodists*; and, like your humble Servant who addresses you, trust them no further than you can see them.

NO HYPOCRITE.

N. B. The Fourth Chapter of Chronicles is received.—A Spanish Ditty; and Letter VI. with all speed.— T. Clayton, Printer, Maidenhead —Price 1d. Oct. 20.

Part of the pamphlet war that marked the non-conformist challenge in Maidenhead.

They Built Jerusalem

The chapel of Saints Andrew and Mary originally came to be through popular demand—
'in compliance with the prayer of the inhabitants'. Bray and Cookham churches were
'dyvers tymes in the yere so surrounded and overflowen wyth water that yr. Highnes seid
subjects cannot passe goe nor travell to their seid churches; by reason whereof the dutie of
yr. seid subjects towards Allmyghtye God hath byn many tymes agnst there wyll left undon'.
The patronage of the church was assumed by the town and under the Elizabeth I Charter
(1582) by the Corporation. The link between church and Corporation was unbroken until
1974, when the Royal Borough of Windsor and Maidenhead came into being.

Before the Victorians began building their substantial churches in the new suburbs—All
Saints' and St Luke's—to colonise the minds of the growing middle classes, the Anglican
community began to lose some of its adherents. There was a ground swell of dissenters.
Its teachers had no status among a population disciplined by the Puritans' observance of
the sabbath. There were rules for the Lord's Day which common folk did well to observe,
such as not riding horses on Sunday. When the Quaker, Thomas Ellwood rode into town
on the sabbath in the spring of 1660 his bridle was seized by the watchman and he was
brought before the Warden as he had no pass from Reading. A couple of years later some
2,000 clergy were ejected from their livings for refusing to accept the Thirty-Nine Articles
and the Book of Common Prayer. But by 1665 the Society of Friends were holding meetings
in Maidenhead. They had connections with the Penn Family who founded Pennsylvania,
USA. A branch lived at Twyford. The Marlow Road Baptist Church had its origins about
this time, in 1672. By 1874 they were meeting above Mr Julius Neve's shop at No. 57 High
Street. He built their first chapel in York Road. The earliest Congregationalist trust deed
is dated 1696. John Cooke was the most notable of the early ministers. There was fire in his
sermons and in at least one of his audiences, who attacked him with lighted straw which
had been dipped in pitch. But he stayed for 43 years. Cooke's principles were the cause of
scurrilous pamphleteering. He, his deacons and supporters in the chapel set objected to
the hiring of strolling players to celebrate the jubilee of George III. He invoked an old
statute declaring them to be rogues and vagabonds. The magistrates were forced to eject
them from the town. Reprisals followed when the pamphleteers dipped their pens in vitriol.
Cooke threatened the printer, T. Clayton, for the pamphlets (selling at a penny) were
circulating as far afield as Marlow—but to no avail.

A few years later, in 1829, John Higgs, who had been living it up 'hand in glove with a
regular fast set', founded the Wesleyan Movement. The first meeting in the Town Hall
brought an outcry from orthodox churchmen. He recruited members from the Congregational church and later a merger with the Countess of Huntingdon's Connexion and the
Primitive Methodists of Queen Street formed the High Street Church to become extremely

influential in town affairs. Higgs, a chemist, bought the old Bear Hotel, No. 35 High Street, and set up the business of Higgs and Walker. Arthur Upson, mayor in 1907, father of Dorothy the novelist, joined the partnership and later ran the business.

Church building boomed in the second half of the 19th century. All Saints, the most notable piece of church architecture in the town, was consecrated in 1857. The first vicar, The Rev Wm Gresley joined Maidenhead's literary tradition by writing a couple of notable novels and other works. St Luke's opened in 1895, and St Peter's, Furze Platt in 1895. Nineteenth century growth quadrupled the population in 50 years.

Roman Catholicism was born out of the first chapel, over doctrinal differences, and the first meetings were at Ives Place in 1867. St Joseph's was erected in 1884.

The former methodist church in Queen Street is now the Citadel of the Salvation Army.

Bombed out Jews in World War I set up a small community in the Ray Park area—between 200-300 of them. Most returned to London after the war. After World War II a reformed synagogue was opened at No. 9 Boyne Hill, through Hugo Schwab, a considerable benefactor to the town. Laurence Misener was variously president, chairman and secretary. There are now about 100 families in the area.

ABOVE: Old engraving of Cookham Church.

BELOW: Bisham Church.

Julius Neve, founder of Neve Brothers April 1874—
and of the Baptist movement locally.

34

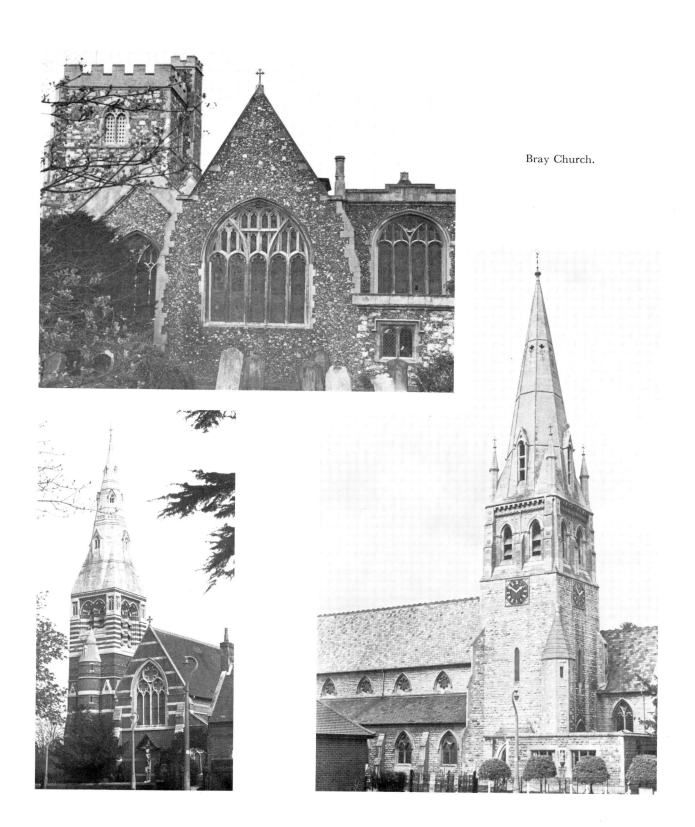

Bray Church.

ABOVE LEFT: All Saint's.
ABOVE RIGHT: St Luke's.

35

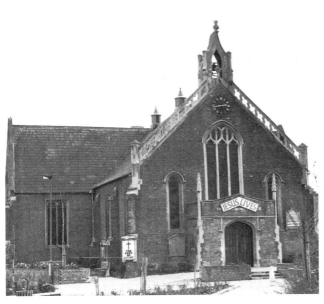

ABOVE: York road Chapel—the Neve achievement.

BELOW LEFT: High street Methodist Church.

BELOW RIGHT: The Baptist Church.

ABOVE LEFT: Shottesbrooke Church—one of the most celebrated Decorated Churches in the country— a cruciform building.

ABOVE RIGHT: Congregational Church.

BELOW LEFT: Stubbings Church.

BELOW RIGHT: Hurley Church, with its timber tower.

ABOVE: St Peter's, Furze Platt.

BELOW LEFT: The Borough Church of St Mary.

BELOW RIGHT: Its predecessor.

38

To the Thames—a Son

Maidenhead town, the 2,123 acres that became the old borough, has a traceable history for about 700 years. It grew up along the roadside where the road itself began a slow rise out of the flood area, on its way into the forest hundreds which were East Berkshire. These were the royal forest lands where in various clearings the nobility of Berkshire lived. Local place names such as Altwood, one of the Queen's woods in Henry VIII's day, date from this time of verderers, woodwards, and musical spellings—Boscos de Ledlegeweyk, for the woods of Littlewick. The longest surviving link with the medieaval sporting kings of Windsor Forest was the Royal Buckhounds. They met for the last time on the Thicket on 11 January, 1911. James I, who was involved in the legendary Vicar of Bray incident, hunted with them.

This road ran along the boundary separating the powerful parishes of Cookham and Bray. It became High Street, Maidenhead, and afterwards, No. 4 in Britain's 20th century hierarchy of trunk roads. Today, still, outside the Bear Hotel, which moved there from No. 35 High Street, the road splays into a bulge, then contracts to squeeze into the narrow High Street. It was in the centre of this bulge that the story of Maidenhead as a town began in the second half of the 13th century. Here, in the middle of the road, astride the parish boundary, was a little piece of holy ground. A tiny chapel of ease to the two parishes was built there in 1269. It was erected for travellers—a place in which to say a prayer for personal safety before attempting to cross the broad, shallow Thames. The bulge was created much later by coach drivers riding high on the box, wheeling their four-in-hands round the church which followed the chapel on this spot. In the heyday of coaching, some 90 a day, as well as local horse-drawn waggons, and gigs turned this spot into the noisiest traffic roundabout since the Irish Dragoons mustered to repel the Prince of Orange.

Some 500 years before the noise of hooves and wheels on High Street cobblestones brought protests to the council, the Hosebond family—they were corn merchants in the City—became interested in converting the chapel into an independent church. Cookham was a long way to walk, and Bray was often in flood.

Permission to set up the church, in 1324, marked the beginning of municipal Maidenhead. But the vicars of Cookham and Bray, and a couple of bishops of Salisbury who threatened excommunication, fought a long delaying action. The vicars were concerned for their loss of income and influence. The final break came after the dissolution of the monasteries. The crown granted a petition. Thus began Maidenhead's first independent church. In 1724 it was rebuilt on the same site. It was moved to the present site in 1824. When the ceiling began falling on the congregation in 1961 the building was condemned. The new church, with its fibreglass spire was consecrated in 1965.

The ferry across the river was replaced by a wooden bridge in 1280, and the Great Western Road was diverted from Cookham to run over it—a sort of Cookham by-pass.

The combination of these two things made Maidenhead a convenient overnight stop on the rocky coach road to Bath. Inn-keepers moved into the High Street; highwaymen moved into the Thicket. There was promise of good business for all with enterprise. Kings, queens, nobility and the quality, were coming this way with purses weighted with gold.

But before the coaching boom began, a man named Thomas Mettyngham became chaplain of the church. It was his initiative which began Maidenhead's political life. An unofficial attempt had been made at the Bridge to collect tolls to pay for repairs. But this was not successful and eventually the Bridge collapsed. Mettyngham set about ways of securing a regular income and the Crown was persuaded to grant the right of tolls. Some of the income came from land at Fourleys (our Forlease). It was probably not difficult to enlist the support of the Crown in this way. The army had an obvious interest in seeing that the bridge stayed put. It was needed for troop movements.

Mettyngham's initiative led to the formation of a guild, authorised in December, 1451, confirming a bequest by John Hosebond for £100 for the formation of a chauntry of St Mary Magdalene in the chapel of St Andrew. St Andrew, appropriately, was the patron saint of fishermen. Fish, especially salmon, was one of the chargeable items for bridge tolls. The guild was called : The Overseer, Warden, Bretheren, and Sisters of the Fraternity or Guild of St Andrew and St Mary Magdalene, Madenhyth, who should maintain Maidenhead Bridge and take tolls. It was 150 years later—7 March, 1582—that Elizabeth I, granted the town its first charter, making it a free town. Authority was given for a market and fairs and a court of Pie Poudre. Civic life began. Under the charter, a warden, who was really the first mayor, bridge-masters, and a council were appointed. This was also the beginning of a locally administered legal system which gave the town some control over fair trading within its boundaries, a sort of right to mind its own business, which grew into our present courts of summary jurisdiction. The bridgemasters, who were also church wardens, linked church and corporation in a unity that was undisturbed until the re-organisation of local government in 1974.

However, the brothers and sisters were not meticulous in their accounting, and there were no newspaper reporters to expose the misappropriation of public funds. The bailiffs and the 'good men of Maidenhead' as the Prior of Bisham called them with an excess of politeness, had 'converted the tolls to their own use'. The Prior was called upon by Henry IV to inquire into the whereabouts of the missing cash.

Misappropriation of bridge funds went on down the years, laying the foundation for the enormous debt that present day ratepayers carry. When the present bridge was opened in 1777, designed by Robert Taylor, who also designed Lincoln's Inn, the Corporation borrowed £19,000 to pay for it. Although, according to Joseph Taylor, whose campaign freed the Bridge in 1903, the Corporation collected £120,000 in tolls, it never paid back the original bond holders. It was a disgraceful piece of management, especially when you turn over the yellowing pages of the old bridgemasters' accounts to find that a lot of this money passed to local inn-keepers for such dignified affairs as 'The Mayor's Feast', and, in 1797, a round of drinks for 330 soldiers, which incidentally cost a mere £5-10s.

Inn-keeping was probably the earliest of the High Street trades. The Bulle was at No. 11 in 1459, the Beare at No. 35 (now the Midland Bank) in 1489, and the White Horse was at the top of High Street from at least 1574. These began as pre-coaching inns because coaching did not begin to thrive until well into the 18th century. One authority gives 1667 as the date of the flying coach from Ludgate Hill to Bath, another that the London-Henley-Wallingford coach of 1704 was the first. Some of the early coaching enterprises failed. Of all the inns, the Greyhound, which was destroyed by fire in 1735, (built on the later site of National Westminster Bank North) was thought to be one of the finest in the land. Evidently, even then the best people were coming this way. It brewed its own beer and had a small farmery stretching across West Street.

It was to the old Beare that James I was said to have wandered when becoming detached from a hunting party. The Vicar of Bray and his curate were eating there. The King had no money, the Vicar refused to help, but the curate paid the King's bill. When the King's identity was revealed he told the prostrate vicar that he would remain vicar of Bray, but he gave a canonry at Windsor to the curate.

The coaching era built up to a crescendo and then the railway stole its business. But before that happened, Maidenhead was a horsey town. The great mail coaches such as the Bristol and Exeter Mail, and the Gloucester Mail, were bringing despatches on a run that had been authorised by Elizabeth I, who started the post as we know it today. It had begun before the coaches and was received here in 1579 by one Robert David. The Queen's order for the Post of Maidenhead allowed him to earn £44.1s.8d for 462 days' service. The first ever parcel post came through Maidenhead.

There was a local coach run by R. Lovegrove, landlord of the Bear; it was a pair-horse coach called the Wonder and claimed to be the fastest of them all, overtaking the four-in-hands, and no doubt, on occasion, turning them into the ditch. In the mid-nineteenth century the Bear yard was full of posters, hunters, ladies' horses, four-in-hands, and drags, and the landlord trained the occasional winner for Maidenhead Racecourse. Vehicles with wheels more than 9 inches wide were not charged tolls because they helped to compact the roads. The road roller had not been invented.

As the coaching era began to fade and the railway to expand in mid-century, the foundations of modern Maidenhead were laid. Men who were to become the pioneers of the High Street, began to move in, modestly at first, but they were to become the town's mayors, and its leading citizenry of the 19th century. Many of their names are still with us. But it was a long slow business replacing the muddy roads with metalled surfaces, draining the streets, and equipping the town with public services. The first crude drainage system was made with wooden pipes out of elm. They were laid in High Street about 1710, but the Corporation's outfall works did not open until 1894. The first street lights were not lit when there was a full moon, and there was a fine on the Gas Company for each lamp not alight on moonless nights. As late as 1912 the council bought two 'liquidity mud carts' for use in cleaning mud off the roads. In dry weather there was a dust problem. Dust was to the 19th century what noise is to the 20th. An alderman of the day said, 'Those of us who use Sunday for its legitimate purpose, trudge through the dust, hot tired, and thirsty to church.' The town had its pious side too.

While serving the nobility and gentry as all the best tradesmen claimed to do, it was the aim of the Victorian shopkeepers to develop the town into a going concern. There was 'a need for houses of a large style to attract new residents who would travel to London, but spend their money in the town'. The Victorians produced a prosperous middle class. Among the lower orders there was widespread poverty which would not disappear until after the second world war. Substantial bequests were still being made in the 19th century to help the poor obtain bread, coal, clothing, and blankets. Maidenhead workhouse dealt with 11,000 tramps a year. Society was not yet ready to regard them as worthy of much help.

When it was pointed out that 40 tramps at the workhouse had only eight towels between them, a member of the Board of Guardians said they did not want to make gentlemen out of them. There was a relief committee in 1892. It met in the police court. When the doors were opened for the dispensing of largesse there were more people outside than there were in the crowded courtroom. They received tickets to collect soup from a vat at Nicholson's Brewery. Jugs, jam and pickle jars were used to carry it away.

Maidenhead became an enclosed place with toll gates on the Bridge, gates at the Thicket, in Braywick Road (as King Street was then called) approximately opposite the southern boundary of the shopping precinct, and a toll gate on Cookham Bridge. Maidenhead became a personalised place within this enclosure. It evolved its own *élite*. Beyond the boundaries were the high cherry lands of Cookham Dean—the fruit was sold at auctions in town—a thousand acres of pastures, thickets, big stands of beech, village greens and commons, running over Winter Hill and gliding into the river valley. The semi-circular sweep of the Thames barred invasion and exploitation as it had done for the men of Wessex centuries before. It was not to be breached until the Development Age. The geophysics of the situation were correct. It made a nice piece of geography.

The birth pangs of the town produced a number of resistance movements. Those who had opposed the arrival of the Great Western Railway were followed by the Anti-Dangerous Motorists' League, anti-vaccinationists, and objectors to the education rate. But the town refused to remain pure. Objectors organised processions, (nowadays called protest marches), through the town, watched by tradesmen's families and apprentices from upstairs windows. J. D. M. Pearce, an ex-mayor and regular speaker against the evils of drink, had this to say about tobacco : 'Smokers have dark, muddy complexions, which are often transferred to their children cheating them out of being good-looking'.

The most spectacular of the resistance movements was the Blue Ribbon Army, a Salvationist group led by a woman—Major Brown. They marched behind a band promoting temperance. But they had opposition—the bibulous Yellow Ribbon Army. Both sides clashed in a pitched battle at Chapel Arches in 1883. Many were injured.

But all was not grim in the process of growing up. There was time to attend Maidenhead Racecourse, which ran from Camley Corner to Tittle Row. It was doing good business and so was cock fighting. In 1828 the Duke of St Albans came to Maidenhead to see a horse owned by John Higgs. Before he started the Methodist movement, Higgs frequented the racecourse, played cricket against the MCC and was a fair shot. Down the years the Methodist Movement has supplied the town with a continuous stream of mayors, magistrates, sobriety, and loyal service. Its members had a lot to do with shaping Victorian Maidenhead.

It was the Victorians who transformed shopping and delivered the produce of the British Empire to the tradesmen's entrance. They built those houses of a large style and set up a code of manners for trade and behaviour which was long to outlast them. But it was the Edwardians who put the town into the gossip columns.

The Charter of Elizabeth I.

43

ABOVE : Old barn at Moor Farm, Holyport.

CENTRE : Bridgemaster's stave. The cap is dated 1667; the royal arms are surmounted by W.R.IIII, and below, the date 1827. It may be the W was painted over an original G (George IV).

BELOW : One of two flagons presented with the chalice in 1657.

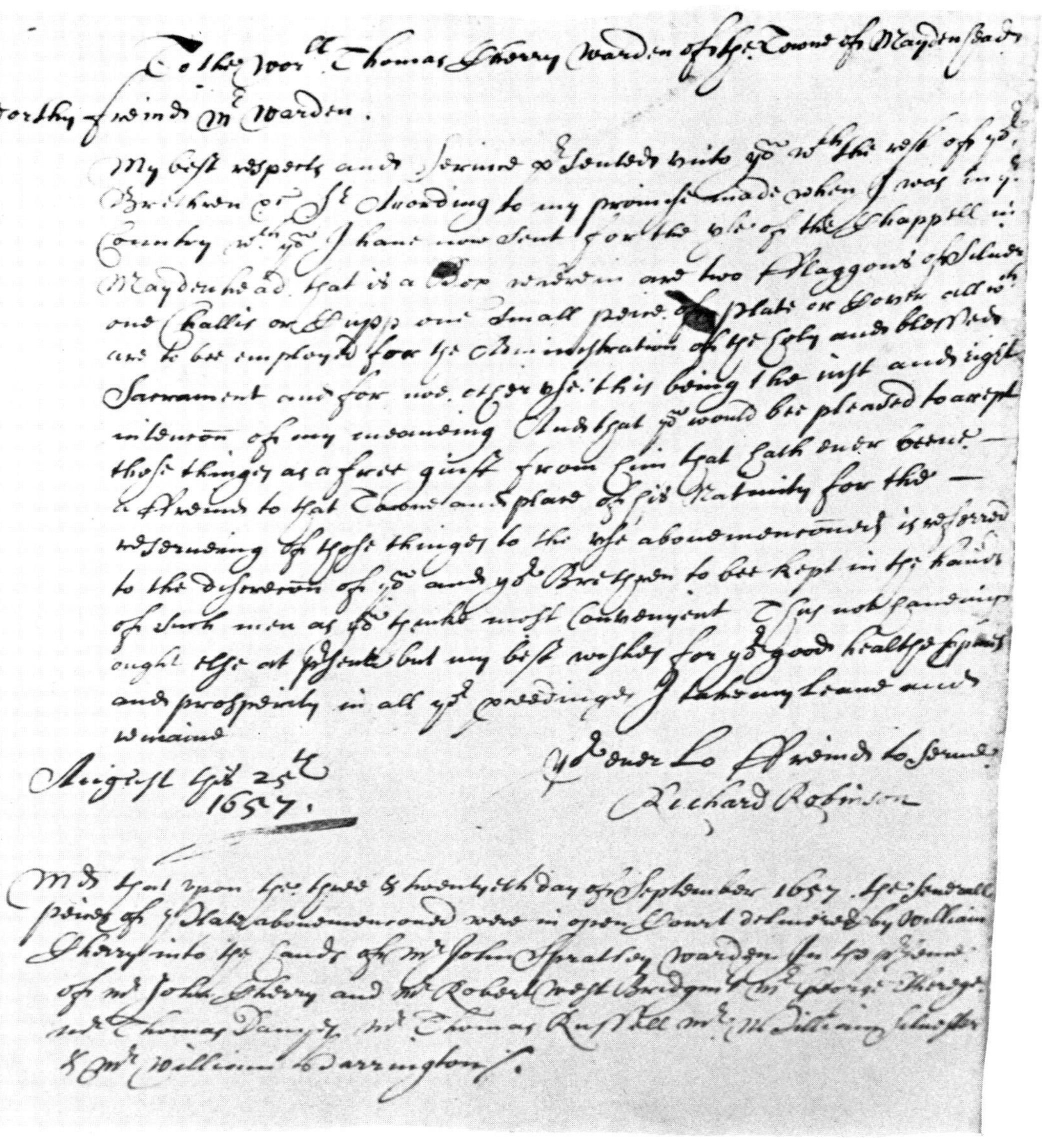

ABOVE: Extract from the Council minute book of 1657.

To the Worshipfull Thomas Cherry Warden of the Towne of Maydenhead. Worthy Freind Mr. Warden,

My best respects and Service presented unto you with the rest of your Brethren etc. According to my promise made when I was in your Country with you I have now sent for the use of the Chappell in Maydenhead that is a Box wherein are two Flaggons of Silver one Challis or Cupp one small peice of Plate or Cover all which are to be employed for the Administration of the holy and blessed Sacrament and for noe other use this being the just and right intention of my meaneing And that you would bee pleased to accept those thinges as a free guift from him that hath ever beene a Freind to that Towne and place of his Nativity for the reserveing of those thinges to the use above mencioned is referred to the discrecion of you and your Brethren to bee kept in the hands of such men as you thinke most Convenyent Thus not haveing ought else at present but my best wishes for your good healthe hapines and prosperity in all your proceedings I take my leave and remaine

August this 25th
1657

Your ever Loving Freind to serve
Richard Robinson

Memorandum that upon the three and twentyeth day of September 1657 the Severall peices of Plate above mencioned were in open Court delivered by William Cherry into the hands of Mr. John Spratley Warden In the presence of Mr. John Cherry and Mr. Robert West Bridgemasters Mr. George Etherege Mr. Thomas Davyes Mr. Thomas Russell Mr. William Silvester & Mr. William Harrington.

46

ABOVE: Maidenhead & Marlow Post Coach, 1780.

BELOW: No 35 High street—originally the Bear Inn,
later Higgs and Walker.

New post office at Hurley!

Jesus Hospital, Bray, drawn by Tony Pickford, Braywick.

MANOR OF COOKHAM,

INCLUDING THE

Parishes of Cookham, Binfield, and Sunninghill,

IN THE COUNTY OF BERKS.

Orders of the COURT LEET and General COURT BARON of HENRY SKRINE, ESQ., Lord of the said Manor, held on the 28th day of November, 1850.

I.   **It is ordered** that the Haywards of this Manor shall receive four pence a head for impounding cattle ; and, if such cattle be brought into the pound by any other person, such other person shall receive two pence a head for the same.

II.   That all manner of cattle turned into the different Commons within this Manor shall be regularly marked with the first letter of the Christian name, and the first letter of the Surname, of the owner or owners of them; and, in case of non-compliance therewith, that the Haywards do impound any cattle found thereon not so marked, and charge one shilling a head for the same.

III.   Several persons having lately made a practice of cutting and carrying away turf from the Commons within this Manor, which is very detrimental to the Inhabitants and Parishioners thereof having right of common, ORDERED that no person, for the future, shall cut or carry away any turf from any of the said Commons, under the penalty of forty shillings per pole, half to the Lord and half to the Hayward.

Pasture, such ass or asses shall be impounded by the respective Haywards, and the owner or owners shall pay five shillings for each ass, for the use of the Hayward ; and, for all stray asses found trespassing on either of the said Commons or Wastes, the Hayward shall receive one shilling per head.

XII.   That no person or persons, whatever, shall make any dung-mine, or lay any manure or compost of any kind, or any timber, wood, bricks, or rubbish, on any of the Commons or Wastes within this Manor, under the penalty of twenty shillings; to be paid half to the Lord of the Manor, and half to the Hayward.

XIII.   That none of the gates against any of the Commons within this Manor shall be taken off or moved away at any period or season of the year; and that the owner or owners of Estates adjoining to the Commons and Wastes within this Manor do keep the fences against all such Commons or Wastes in good and sufficient repair at all times of the year ; and that the Haywards do inspect and report the same to the Foreman of the last Leet Jury, who is thereupon to make his report to the Steward; and that the owner or owners of lands do, at all times, well and sufficiently scour,

ABOVE : Handbill for the Manor of Cookham.
(Courtesy Tom Clifton).

48

MAIDENHEAD RACES.

TUESDAY, October 10, 1775.

The Ladies Purse of Fifty Pounds, *(the beſt of Three Four-Mile Heats) by any Horſe, Mare or Gelding ; Five Year Olds, to carry 8ſt. 8lb. Six Year Olds, to carry 8ſt. 12lb. and Aged Horſes to carry 9ſt. 3lb. Thoſe that have won one 50l. Plate this Year to carry 3lb. extraordinary, thoſe that have won two 50l. Plates this Year, to carry 5lb. extraordinary, and thoſe that have won three or more 50l. Plates this Year, to carry 7lb. extraordinary.*

Horse	RIDER's Names and the Colours of their Dreſs.	1ſt Heat.	2d Heat.	3d Heat.
MR. Brown's br. horſe, Crony, aged, (3 plates 9ſt. 10lb.	William Barnes, Blue.	2	2	
Mr Rider's bay gelding, Caſca, 6 years old, 8ſt. 12lb.	John Rider, Purple.	dif.		
Mr. Gwyn's ch. h. Culprit, 6 years old, (1 plate) 9ſt. 1lb.	Rider unknown.	4	dr.	
Mr. Jennings's bay horſe, Neſtor, aged, (2 plates) 9ſt. 8lb.	Thomas Garret, Orange.	3	4	
Mr. Dymock's bay horſe, Zachary, aged, 9ſt. 3lb	J Reynard, Blue & White.	6	dr.	
Mr. Stacey's Fortune Hunter, 5 yrs. old, (2 plates) 8ſt. 13lb.	R. Lefenby, Bl & White.	1	1	
Capt. O'Kelly's b. h. Caſſimus, 5 years old, (1 plate) 8ſt. 11lb.	Samuel Merrit, Red.	5	3	

WEDNESDAY, October 11.

The TOWN Purse of Fifty Pounds *(the beſt of three Two Mile Heats) by any Horſe, &c not exceeding Four Years old laſt Graſs ; Colts to carry 8ſt. 4lb. and Fillies 8ſt. 0 lb. and thoſe that have won one 50l. Plate this Year to carry 4lb. extraordinary, thoſe that have won two 50l. Plates this Year, to carry 7lb. extraordinary, and thoſe that have won three or more 50l. Plates this Year, to carry 10lb. extraordinary.*

Horse	RIDER's Names and the Colours of their Dreſs.	1ſt Heat.	2d Heat.	3d Heat.
LORD Caſtlehaven's grey colt, Boſphorus, 8ſt. 4lb.	Edmund Allen, Red.			
Mr. Adams's dun colt, Dunny : 2 plates ; 8ſt. 11lb.	William Briſtow, Crimſon.			
Mr. Green's bay colt, Trimmer, 8ſt. 4lb.	John South, Yellow.			
Mr. Duggins's bay colt, Lightfoot, (one plate) 8ſt. 8lb.	William Barnes, Striped.			
Mr. Tomb's bay colt, Codrus, (one plate) 8ſt. 8lb.	Unknown.			
Mr. Stephenſons's grey colt, (to be ſold) 8ſt. 4lb.	Unknown.			
Mr. Rider's black colt, Ivory Black, 8ſt. 4lb.	John Talbot, Purple,			
Mr. Langbridge's grey colt, Burntcruſt, 8ſt. 4lb.	John Brown, Yellow.			
Capt. Bertie's bay filley, Lady Catchet, 8ſt.	William Blois, Yellow.			
Capt. O'Kelly's cheſnut filley, Juno, 8ſt.	Giles Edwards, Red.			

THURSDAY, October 12

The NOBLEMEN and GENTLEMENS Subscription Purse of Fifty Pounds, *Give and take, free for any Horſe, &c. Aged Horſes of 14 Hands to carry 8ſt. 7lb., and to allow 7lb. for every Year under ; and to carry 3 lb. extraordinary for every Plate they ſhall have won this Year.*

Horse	RIDER's Names and the Colours of their Dreſs.	1ſt Heat.	2d Heat.	3d Heat.
MR. Tilbury's grey mare, Meliſſa, 6 years old, (1 plate) 13 hands, 3 inches, 1-half, 1-8th.—8ſt. 0lb. 6z.	Thomas Campbell, White.			
Mr. Watts's bay horſe, Gudgeon, aged, 14h.—8ſt. 7lb.	William Griſton, Crimſon.			

*** To ſtart at One o'Clock.

49

ABOVE: Bray's first fire engine.

BELOW: Hare and Hounds, Braywick road, corner of
Harvest Hill road.

50

TO THE
BURGESSES
Of the Borough of Maidenhead.

1. If we get **FUSSY** in, will he guarantee to attend to the business of the town the same as he does to his own? I hope he will.

2. Will **WIRE** guarantee us no floods this year, so that we can go occasionally to his hospitable mansion (the Hall) by the sea, and have some tea; we can invite the temperance band.

3. Supposing we build a new Brewery for the benefit of the Rate-payers, will the **THREE-YEAR-OLD LAME MARE** guarantee not to kick up a row if the new proprietor gives a free entertainment at the completion of the same? We will undertake to drink beer only. No Policemen admitted.

4. Will the **BOATMAN** guarantee we Ratepayers boats during the season free of charge?

5. Will the **RETIRED SCORER** still officiate in his old capacity? If so, we shall expect him to put us up good scores when we play in any matches.

6. Will **DONE BROWN** give us meat for nothing? If so, he is the man for us.

7. Will **POOR BARKS** agree with the great seed merchants to supply all working men, next Spring, with seed potatoes that will not go bad at lifting up time?

8. Will the **DRAPER DEALER** guarantee us pocket handker-chiefs (which he sells cheap from bankrupt stocks), not to fall to pieces in our hands when we blow our nose?

9. Will **FOXEY** guarantee not to act as his name warrants, but be civil, and not take any notice of his fellow ratepayers' business.

If the above will guarantee us these privileges, we will run them in.

To the Point.—Why did the proposed dinner over the Badge and Chain fall through? Was it because of the prosecution at the late Berkshire Brewery Banquet; or is it through the fault of the subscrib-ers to the Badge not paying up in time? or is it through the poorness of the chief movers, not being able to pay their shot for a banquet?

Borough election fun!

51

ABOVE: Brunel's Sounding Arch—largest single brick span in Europe.

BELOW: Widening the arch.

POOLE'S & RING'S
CHARITIES.

NOTICE IS HEREBY GIVEN THAT THE

FLANNEL & COATS

from these Charities will be distributed to the
Poor at the Market Room under the Town
Hall, on Tuesday, the 20th of December, at
Three o'clock in the Afternoon.

FRED. T. WARD,

Maidenhead, 16th December, 1870.

Clerk.

ABOVE: Charity notice.

BELOW: The Tollgate and Bridge House.

ABOVE: J. D. M. Pearce, a Maidonian and a Victorian city father.

LEFT and RIGHT: Police truncheons.

BELOW: The old Guildhall.

54

A last look at Edward's forge in Park street,
at Broadway corner.

An early boundary map: in 1835 there was only one street, only the gas works and 3 houses across the bridge. North Town contained 150 houses.

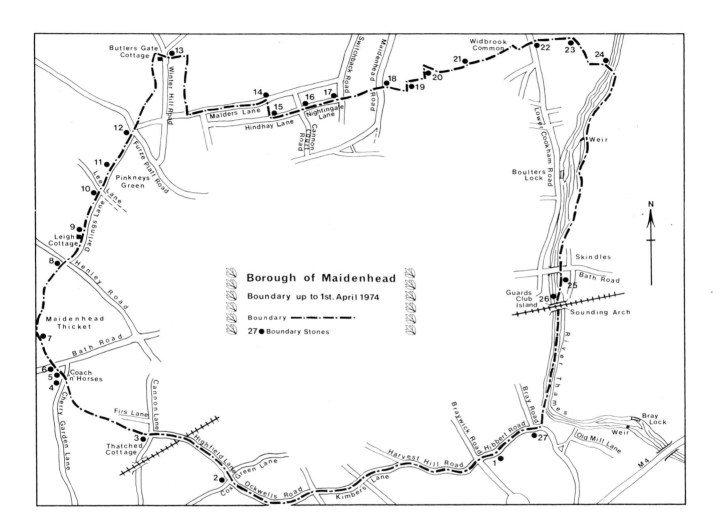

The Borough boundaries—up to the creation of the new Royal Borough
in 1974. This was the final shape of Maidenhead, the town. (Redrawn by
Tony Pickford from original by Peter Nevell).

ABOVE: On Guard at the railway bridge.

BELOW: Leaving for France—all World War I. (Courtesy Malcolm Peake).

War Haven

Only 1,650 bombs fell in the Maidenhead area in the 1939-45 war; of these 1,500 were incendiaries. One Doodle Bug (flying bomb) fell in a garden off Cookham Road. The town was undamaged. Sixty-two people were slightly injured in air raids, and one man, sitting by his fireside at Furze Platt, had his leg broken when an unfused bomb came through his roof. In terms of the South East, Maidenhead was a safe area. That was why treasures from the London museums were stored here, at Knowl Hill, and why foreign royalty were among our evacuees. But Maidenhead earned its place in history in this war for another reason. It was the headquarters of the Air Transport Auxiliary (ATA), that phantom force of civilians in uniform who ferried 308,567 war planes of all kinds to their battle stations. Young girls in their early twenties were flying unarmed four-engined bombers in fair weather and foul, day and night, to keep the fighting squadrons supplied. Flight Captain Miss Joan Hughes, at 22, had 600 flying hours behind her and was instructing on all types of aircraft. The volunteer pilots included Jim Mollison who lived in the district after the war and his wife Amy Johnson, both international flyers, and volunteers from all over the world— Australia, New Zealand, Chile, Poland, Canada, USA, Denmark, Austria, Belgium, India, Czechoslovakia, Ethiopia, and Holland. They lost 154 air crew, including one Air Training Corps cadet. Maidenhead women broke in horses for the army in 1914-18.

In one sense the town saw more of the first war than of the second, because of the train loads of casualties. Viscount Astor built Cliveden Hospital in his grounds and gave it to the Canadian Army. It was supervised by his wife Nancy Astor; 24,000 men passed through it. It was rebuilt as the Canadian Red Cross Memorial Hospital. Maidenhead Cottage Hospital was turned over to war wounded, dealing with a constant stream from the front.

First 1914 evacuees came from Belgium, some 130 of them. In 1917, 2,000 Londoners came to Maidenhead to escape air raids. Some walked all the way carrying mattresses and feather beds. But in 1939, evacuation of school children from London was organised on a massive scale. Some 6,000 children, mothers, and expectant mothers arrived in the first wave. There followed two residential schools and their staffs. All were placed in private homes. The Women's Voluntary Service handled this complex problem. The town's most distinguished evacuee was Queen Whilhelmina of Holland. It was arranged through the firm of Hillier Parker May and Rowden, the estate agents. When the Dutch Prime Minister called there he met E. Norman Vooght of Maidenhead. The Prime Minister became interested in this Dutch name and Mr Vooght arranged the Queen's stay at Stubbings House. King Haakon of Norway moved to Folijohn Park, Fifield.

Both wars brought German prisoners to the area. In 1914-18 there was a camp for officers at Holyport, and in 1939-45 a POW camp at Kimbers, near the M4 footbridge. Large numbers of troops were stationed here for short periods in both wars. The Showboat in

Oldfield Road, gay night spot of the club era between the wars, became a services club—a landing strip for Americans and the Air Transport Auxiliary.

Lord Desborough used part of Taplow Court as a rest centre for nurses in 1914-18 and he organised a local defence force for Taplow. Anti-parachute patrols on land and on the river were normal Home Guard duties in 1939-45. Food shortages in both wars were felt. The council ran a soup kitchen—penny a bowl—at the old Britannia (No. 91 High Street) and ex-Prime Minister Asquith was refused a second slice of bread at Skindles during the first world war. In 1939-45 a British Restaurant was opened where the Town Hall now stands. At the height of the blitz, local firemen assisted the London Fire Brigade and were in fact a mobile force travelling wherever duty called.

Geoffrey Messum of Bray was among local boat owners who joined the fleet of little ships which sailed to Dunkirk to help evacuate the BEF. He brought back 22 Frenchmen and one Englishman. The WVS services canteen served 3,000,000 men and among its visitors was Princess Juliana who was staying with her mother at Stubbings. As soon as Holland was liberated Maidenhead WVS brought Dutch children here to recuperate from the horrors of war. They also supplied clothing to the hard-pressed people of Caen.

Out of the mixing bowl of war came new people who settled here. The old ATA field became Fairey Aviation's workshop. They built the Rotodyne, the world's first helicopter airliner there. Fairey Surveys flew from the field to remap large areas of the world. The Duke of Edinburgh learned to fly there, and Flight Captain Miss Joan Hughes, with no more bombers to ferry, became instructor at West London Aero Club.

The war left a massive housing shortage and serious overcrowding. A plaque in the Town Hall remembers those who died in the earlier Boer War, but the man who invented and trained the famous City of London Imperial Volunteers, came from Maidenhead—Colonel Sir Charles Gervase Boxall, of Battlemead.

Duchess of Kent with WVS workers and some of the
lads outside the St Ives Hotel canteen.

ABOVE: Civil Defence Platoon, Maidenhead Home Guard Battalion, World War II.

BELOW: Officers of the 2nd Berks (Maidenhead) Home Guard Battalion.

61

ABOVE: Maidenhead Bridge in 1810.

BELOW: The river at Bray.

Down by the Riverside

From the beginning, Maidenhead has been both a mooring and a point of disembarkation from boats from across the sea, because of the Thames. The first arrivals came to fight and to trade. The river became a busy trade route for heavy transport long before fashion and pleasure claimed it. Supplies of all kinds went by barge. The boat came before the coach or carriage. And industry began at the riverside with the mills. The best known place on the Middle Thames takes its name from the milling trade—Boulters Lock. Boulting was a milling term.

Boulters is not the most beautiful lock on the river but it is the most famous. It has been well-known from at least 1746. Then it was the first lock on the Thames above London Bridge. The Lock was named after the mill, originally Ray Mill Lock. The mill was named after the family who ran it—Ray—and was probably built on the site of a much older mill that ground corn for the Roman legions. The name 'Ray' is said to derive from a Saxon word meaning a stream. Ray Mill was one of 28 mills between Oxford and Staines, almost all of which are as ancient as Domesday. Richard Ray became the first lock-keeper. He was appointed in February, 1773. Previously the lock was run by the miller, and in 1746 had been attached to the Bucks bank. Previously it was what was called a 'flash' lock. Flash locks built a head of water by the insertion of planks in the stream. They were highly dangerous. Barges plunged over the weir often with loss of life and cargo.

All obstructions to the navigable river, including weirs, were declared illegal. Richard I, Magna Charta, Edward III, all declared they should be removed. Edward III also ordered his sheriffs to pull down the mills and anything else 'originating in the greed of man'. The object of all the early Acts was to protect those using the river from those owning the land on the banks. But the Acts were ignored. Even Maidenhead Bridge obstructed navigation because barges had to lower their masts to pass beneath it. Some landowners charged for the use of the tow path. The history of river management up to the early days of the Thames Conservancy is of the gradual erosion of public rights, both upon the river and upon its banks. Parliament constantly tried to keep the Thames a free highway. In 1695 an Act was passed 'to prevent the exactions of the occupiers of locks and weares upon the River Thames westwards and for ascerteyning the rates of water carriage upon the said river'. The Act stipulated that locks had to be marked for a flash so that the height of water could be examined. It also stipulated that a boat and sufficient tackle and a winch in good repair be kept at every lock.

From 1197 to 1857 the City of London exercised a vague authority over the Thames. It was strict as far as Staines. Oxford had its own commission. Maidenhead reaches were left to their own devices. Powerful riparian owners filled the vacuum. One of these was the Earl of Orkney of Taplow Court. He was one of Marlborough's generals at the Battle of Blenheim. The Thames Conservancy came into existence in 1857.

By the mid-eighteenth century barges were hauling more than 69,000 tons of goods upstream annually. The pressure at Boulters was too heavy for the lock when the barge traffic began to build up. It was worn out by 1826 and a new lock was built on the present site about three years later. This was rebuilt into the one we recognise today and opened by Lord Desborough in 1912. It is still the largest lock on the river. The barges, often more than 60ft. long, were either towed upstream by horses, travelled lazily under sail, or were hauled manually. When the towpath ended on one side, due to the riparian owner having taken possession of the path, the haul was continued from the other bank. The original ferries, such as My Lady Ferry at Cliveden Reach, were for transferring barge horses. Anyone not concerned in navigation was forbidden to use them.

There was stabling for these horses and accommodation for bargemen near Boulters, on the site of which was built the fashionable Ray Mead Hotel. The use of horses for towing continued into the 1920s.

River affairs on this stretch of water have had a dominant influence upon the town. From the mid-eighteenth century when the decline in barge traffic began, an interest in recreational pursuits started, aided by a number of adventurous sportsmen and others. Where man once fished for food he now fished for pleasure. The barges of trade gave way to cruising. More people came to live by the river for this reason. The town began to grow and changes which were to affect the whole ecology of the riverside were put in motion. In the heyday of the barges the Upper Thames was a rural world of simple husbandry. The barge folk were a separate community of itinerant people. There was a rich harvest from the Thames in salmon and trout. Grig-weels—wicker baskets made from Thames-side osier beds—were sunk in the river to catch eels. They were the forerunners of the eel bucks (baskets) which were mechanically operated on a frame, and permanent structures.

The arrival of the Great Western Railway speeded the change in the nature of the riverside. This opened in 1838. In some respects the GWR began at Maidenhead. The wooden sleepers for the track were delivered to Maidenhead by barge and plunged into large tanks of preservative near the Bridge. Daniel Gooch's famous North Star—the locomotive that pulled the first train—was delivered to Maidenhead by barge. It has lent its name to various public houses. The first stretch of line terminated at Maidenhead's Dumb Bell Station, Taplow, just a few steps from the river. The fare by open carriage from Paddington was 3s 6d. The comfort of a 1st class posting carriage cost 6s 6d. London was growing and so was the tourist trade.

But the growing towns were discharging their effluent into the Thames. The salmon left, followed shortly by the trout. The last salmon was caught in Boulters in 1821.

It was the arrival of the excursionists and playground people which caused a number of questions to be asked. Why had the banks been enclosed by private landowners? Why must you pay to moor? What had happened to the free passage on the Thames highway? Why were backwaters chained off? By whose authority? A Select Committee of the House of Commons met in 1885 to thrash all these matters out. In view of current proposals for a Thames Walk scheme along the towpaths, the Committee's findings make interesting reading today. It reported that the public had rights to move boats over every part of the river as an ancient and free highway and urged the importance of establishing a free towing path, to be used as a footpath, throughout the navigated length of the Thames. But none of this was to be done.

Sir Gilbert Clayton-East, a conservator, who gave evidence before the Select Committee, was described by the Chairman as 'the very stern champion of riparian ownership'. As the Conservancy's funds came from the public, conservators were expected to champion public rights. He also stated that there was no such thing as a public landing place in the Upper Thames. Referring to Maidenhead, he said, 'There is nowhere they could land except at a boat builder's unless they went some way up the Cut and then the conservators would interfere with them'. Sir Gilbert added that if they moored on the towing path, they would have to pay a fee or a fine.

The change from the working river was seen along the banks in the arrival of new boat-houses, one of the earliest of these set up by the Andrews family. Boat building became an important if small industry. Local craftsmen built craft for export all over the world. The Andrews family were also renowned as professional fishermen. In the days when you hired a boat and a waterman to go with it, the sportsman hired a boat and a fisherman to go with it. The Wilder family was also closely identified with this era. Anthony Wilder was in the charge of the Light Brigade—and so incidentally was Sir Roger Palmer who lived across the stream at Glen Island—but along Thames-side the name Wilder meant watermen and professional fishermen. The Fishing Gazatte of 1890 described Ned Andrews, who was born in 1846, as one of the cleverest fresh water fishermen of his day. 'Four generations of the family have been famous fishermen at Maidenhead'. Ned was also champion professional puntsman of the Thames, and his father was 'the finest rod and line fisherman ever known'. His grandfather is thought to have been the first man in Maidenhead to have let boats for pleasure. He founded the firm of E. Andrews and Son.

There was a trout fishing season in Maidenhead and the Advertiser reported the catches. For instance, in April, 1882, Captain Haynes, attended by Harry Wilder, landed a 7lb. trout. But changes were coming quickly. Amateur oarsmen were signalling the arrival of a new age. It had its beginning with feats of rowing prowess.

One of the great all-time rowing feats occurred in the 1820s. Viscount Newry and five of his servants, all Maidenhead and Cookham men, accepted a wager for a timed row to Westminster Bridge. They beat the clock in 18 hours to win the bet. The Oxford University crew used to train on Maidenhead reaches and on one occasion put on a concert for a village show at Cookham. The first university boat race was rowed at Henley in 1829.

These early days produced another man whose name was to become a household word along the river—Jonathan Bond. He reclaimed the swampy land adjoining the Bridge in River Road, Taplow, and built a boathouse on it. At busy times he employed 40 hands. He built a remarkable vehicle called a shallop. This was a horse-drawn houseboat-cum-barge, a sort of link between the old days and the new. Edward VII was once taken to Cliveden in it.

Presumably, because Jonathan Bond made a good job of his boathouse the Corporation asserted its rights to ownership of the land. The leases of this and other plots used to be put up for auction. In 1891, when Jonathan paid £250 a year for his lease the auction was attended by boat letters and boat builders from all along the river.

Another kind of traffic began to ply regularly in the wake of the barges, carrying both cargo and passengers, this was the river steamer. They began the excursion trade into the riverside community. The first of the Salters Fleet, the Alaska, was built by the Horsham family at their Bourne End yard. The family is still in the boat business at Boulters Lock. In 1870 there were six steamers coming through Maidenhead on a daily service to Oxford. Three of them—Kingston, Windsor, and Cliveden—were shipped abroad in World War I.

The Cliveden was sunk in the Mediterranean. It was replaced by the second Cliveden running today. In 1866 it took five days for the Alaska to steam from Oxford to Kingston.

Another branch of the recreation and entertainment business to become especially associated with Maidenhead made an inconspicuous beginning in Mill Lane, Taplow, unknown even to itself. It was a little inn called the Orkney Arms. On December 23, 1743 the Corporation leased to Mr John March one and twenty foot of their ground at the annual rent of 20 shillings, to make a way to his inn. The Orkney Arms was to be run, eventually, by William Skindle. It developed into Thames-side's best known hotel, fostering almost a cult in elegant riverside happenings. Its neighbour became the Brigade of Guards Boat Club which is commemorated by a plaque on the present hotel building. The Guards' Club later moved to the west bank below the Riviera Hotel's site. Such was the nostalgia among the officer classes during service in France in World War I that a second Skindles came into being at Popperinge, Belgium. It is now proposed to demolish Skindles, erect riverside homes on the site, and put the restaurant back in the middle of the development.

The Thames at Maidenhead became the place to go and you were expected to dress for the occasion. Flannels, blazers and boaters, tea on Skindles lawn, champagne picnics, pretty girls in skiffs, pageants, regattas, and Venetian fêtes, were all the rage. Much the same was happening in other riverside towns, but in Maidenhead there was a significant difference. It managed to cream off all the best people for three good reasons—Taplow Court, Cliveden (which was once part of Taplow Court Estate), and the Guards Club, which had a commodious ballroom.

The two big houses entertained kings, queens, dukes of the royal blood, ambassadors, prime ministers in dozens, writers, actors, generals, and the world famous by the score. They made history as well as fun. This gave Maidenhead a cosmopolitan air. The regular flow of assorted high society from Europe and America washed over the town on its way to Taplow, and some of them were occasionally seen in the High Street. The town basked in the glory of it all. A river season grew up around these people, which culminated in the Ascot Sunday parade of boats at Boulters. Socially, no one could afford to miss it. The Guards Club ball, sometimes attracting royal princesses, was part of it. Mothers with eligible daughters moved in for the season, gave parties in their resplendent drawing-rooms, and groomed their daughters for a bloodless conquest of the Brigade of Guards.

Thousands crowded the river bank to watch the high tide of society flowing past Ray Mead Road. Fashionable London turned Maidenhead into Mayfair-by-the-Thames. Boulters became as well-known as any beauty spot. Lock-keeper Turner was quoted on river matters in London newspapers and magazines. In the throng, the insignia of famous Thames boating clubs could be observed on blazer pockets and hatbands, and there was the occasional soldier of the Empire. Royalty and statesmen purred past the promenade in electric launches. Lesser fry punted and skiffed. Good manners and fashion abounded. The stars, as well as the girls from the back row of the chorus, found themselves at Maidenhead in the best of company, and the big houses were lit up late in more ways than one. Eventually, the hotels, aided and abetted by a few fashionable riverside clubs, notably Murrays and the Hungaria, made riverside gaiety possible for the better-off for twelve months of the year.

The arrival of the famous at Taplow Court had an unusual beginning. During the reign of Mary I there was a state prison there, but only for VIPs. They were among our most distinguished residents. But there had been several others before the influx of Victorian notables.

66

By 1740, Fredrick Prince of Wales, father of George III, was installed in Cliveden. He appears not to have made a good impression on the district, but he was responsible for an historic musical interlude in 1740, which, like the Orkney Arms, was to become rather well-known. He commissioned the first performance of Dr Arne's Rule Britannia, which was performed in Cliveden's Rustic Theatre, a green plateau with trees for flats, overlooking the Thames. Frederick died in 1751 after being struck by a ball while playing cricket at Cliveden.

The grounds of Cliveden were to be made into what was described as 'among the most beautiful grounds in the land' by the beautiful Duchess of Sutherland, one of whose frequent visitors was Queen Victoria.

The grounds of Taplow Court were equally splendid and included an avenue of trees planted by the crowned heads of Europe: a royal arboretum. Royalty appeared to use the Thames at Maidenhead as common folk were to use the 'buses. A typical upper crust party of 1891 assembled on the lawn of the George Inn, Bray (now the Waterside) on July 17, bound for Henley Royal Regatta. Two of Teggs steam launches were moored at the landing stage decorated with marguerites and calceolarias. Their scarlet awnings gleamed in the sunshine. On the lawn were the Prince of Wales, the Duke of Edinburgh, and the Duke of Clarence and Avondale. They had been waiting for the Kaiser to join them for an hour and were a little restless. He had a cold and failed to turn up.

Lady Desborough, queen of wit and fashion, presided over the famous Taplow Court parties. Big parties continued there up to 1939. There was a succession of Saturday-to-Monday parties, water parties, and fancy dress balls. At the water parties all sorts of top drawer people were apt to be taken down a peg. In 1904 Winston Churchill was flung into the river while wearing greatcoat, top hat, and spats. Lady Desborough wrote of the incident, 'He swam very composedly'. He went in again during a water fight five years later. At another party, 150 colonial premiers and their wives were entertained. Looking back on these fabulous events shortly before she died, Lady Desborough remarked, 'We did have fun'.

Thames-side's most dynamic hostess was Lady Nancy Astor, first woman MP, whose visitors' list ranged from George Bernard Shaw to the so-called Cliveden Set of the 1930s, which favoured appeasement with Germany. Lord Astor used his house and grounds as a meeting place for both national and local government personalities. He followed Lord Desborough as High Steward of Maidenhead. He was succeeded in this office by his son. The last of the Cliveden parties is remembered in modern history as the Profumo affair. Of all the people who attended these parties none was more revered and admired than Lord Desborough himself, one of the greatest Englishmen of his day. He became the first chairman of the Thames Conservancy, beginning an epoch in river history in which he concentrated upon improving navigation.

All the people who lived by the river were involved in its affairs and in broad terms formed a community with a common interest. Lord Desborough may have been chairman of the Conservancy, but along the river he was thought of as amateur champion puntsman of the Thames.

Until World War II, Ascot Sunday was still the social event of the year. In June, 1932, British Movitone News put it on the super cinema circuit. Some 12,210 vehicles had come over Maidenhead Bridge, bringing people to see the spectacle. The lock and promenade were crowded and from the water drifted music from boat-borne gramophones. At 3 pm

Salters Empress of India, appropriate for the Empire visitors present, passed through the lock with the passengers singing Glory, Glory, Alleluia. Handsome launches and punts were everywhere. Mr and Mrs George Mattingley were punted by their daughter Nora, former lady champion. Conspicuous among the larger craft was the Lady Frainy with Sir Dhunjibhoy Bomanji of Oakley Court on board with a large party of Indian friends. The Advertiser described this 'most luxurious private launch' on the Upper Thames as 'a beautiful creation in immaculate white with a gorgeous canopy'. Mr G. L. Waldron's big launch with saloon tables set and waiters in attendance, was also in the parade.

But Ascot Sunday has gone. Its splendour was repeated in Edwardian costume in 1951, a flamboyant show of nostalgia for the Festival of Britain watched by some 20,000 people. Cicelie Courtnidge fell in the river when the landing stage at Ray Mill Island collapsed.

After World War II the community became less well-defined. The boatyards chopped up their punts, the punting regatta moved away and the power boats took over. The steamers converted to diesel. Fashionable philandering and camping Jerome K. Jerome style in hooped punts were things of the past. The riverside was redeveloped for people desperate for homes. The Guards Club fell to the demolition men. Just every once in a while the river asserts its rights over attempts to municipalise it.

When the disastrous floods of 1947 poured over the flood plain, full scale relief measures were in force for marooned families. Some 120 were evacuated to the Town Hall and the Army moved in to aid the distressed. Funds were sent from all parts of the Commonwealth to help repair the damage to homes, and the Lord Mayor of London, whose fund also helped, came personally to inspect the damage. Maidenhead sponsored a conference of Thames mayors from which came the Flood Ditch Scheme. It carries flood water from Blackamoor Lane to Bray and protects the town.

Changes in municipal government have left the authorities without the feel of the river community. The hereditary element is missing from both the community and the council, whose responsibility is to landscape Thames-side without harming it and understand its river moods. High ground Maidenhead is inclined to put the river out of mind. The riverside was where a lot of people went who ought not to be there unchaperoned. But the river keeps a lot of its pageantry in spite of power boats. The Queen's Swan Master, John Turk of Cookham, presides over the annual Swan Upping ceremony. Its beginnings were in mediaeval times. The swans belong to the Queen or the Dyers and Vintners Companies and swan upping is concerned with marking them.

Boatbuilding firms still export their beautiful craftsmanship all over the world. The scullers from Maidenhead Rowing Club are still on the water. The transistorised radio has outdated the gramophone and there is a different noise in the lock cut, from power boats, while the big jets roar overhead. But something of the traditional fun of sauntering by the river is preserved by the council in Bridge Gardens and Ray Mill Island, Thames-side's most beautiful public park. They are an encouragement to light-hearted thoughts and time-wasting pursuits purely for pleasure.

The beginning of the new era for Thames-side took place on October 18, 1974, when Queen Elizabeth II made her historic Thames journey through her new Royal Borough of Windsor and Maidenhead. It was barely six months before, that Maidenhead's first charter, granted by Elizabeth I, was surrendered to the archives. It was the first time that any monarch had ever made such a journey on the Thames.

Boulters Lock and Ray Mill House, by
Edmund John Nieman (1813-1876).

CENTRE: Cookham Dean Bottom.
BELOW: Cookham ferry.

69

LEFT: Boulters Lock, 1898 (note old bridge). (F. Franklyn)

ABOVE RIGHT: Boat rollers at Boulters—to bypass the lock.

Regatta crowds.

BELOW RIGHT: Punting supplies to the marooned in the 1900 floods.

70

ABOVE : Summer day at Boulters.

BELOW : Ascot Sunday as it used to be.

71

ABOVE: The 1894 floods in Ray street.

BELOW LEFT: Dr Plumb drives through Bridge road, regardless.

BELOW RIGHT: Botany Bay (above the Boulters Weir).

ABOVE: Club outing by steam, by golly.

BELOW: Steam launch before Bridge House (now Bridge Gardens).

ABOVE : Thames Hotel.

LEFT : Horsham's Bourne End yard, whence the first
Salter's steamer came. (Sidney Horsham).

John Turk of Cookham, Queen's Swan Master.

Swan-Uppers corner a cygnet.

Maidenhead Bridge with Bridge House, afterwards Murrays Club.

INSET TOP ABOVE : Mr Turner, famous keeper of Boulters Lock.

INSET BELOW : J. Bond—designer and builder of steam launches.

Among those Present

Traditional Maidenhead was created by a vibrant mixture of people, many of whom were exceptionally talented. They landscaped it, gave it the colour of Pinkneys Green clay, and although some gave no more than laughter, it was heard in the Haymarket, Lyceum, and Drury Lane theatres. They began its links with the theatre and the arts, and brought kings and queens here to enjoy themselves at the week-ends.

From Geys Manor, Holyport, came the founder of the Bodleian Library, Oxford, Sir Thomas Bodley. The editor of Leland's papers, which were compiled for Henry VIII, was Thomas Hearne (1678-1735) of Shottesbrooke. The seafaring Pococks of Ray Lodge produced a number of painters, including Isaac Pocock whose Murder of Thomas A'Beckett won the Royal Institution's 100 guinea prize. From Cookham came Fredrick Walker. His Harbour of Refuge (Jesus Hospital, Bray) is in the Tate Gallery. The amazing Spencers of Cookham included painters and musicians, especially Stanley Spencer who is probably the only English artist with a permanent gallery of his works on view in his own village, and his younger brother Gilbert.

From Fieldhead, Bourne End, came the famous editor of the old Daily News and member of Punch's staff, John Lehmann. In later years the first colour cover for Punch was to be drawn by Eric Burgin, who went to Gordon Road School, and became the first British cartoonist to have a one-man show in New York after the second world war. The Mayoress of 1907 became the top selling romantic novelist of her day. The Robinson family of Cookham had Heath Robinson for an uncle, and their father illustrated the works of Robert Louis Stevenson.

Radio and television brought an influx of the well-known to town, including the late Richard Dimbleby, who lived for a time at Mill Head, Boulters Island.

Into the mixture went diplomats, diamond merchants, and rich men who enjoyed Maidenhead's principal industry—pleasure. The diplomats included Sir Berry Cusack-Smith of Redlands, a local JP and former Consul General Valparaiso and Charge d'Affairs Santiago, Abram Hoffnung of Rawdon Hall, Holyport, Hawaiian Charge d'Affairs. The Belgian Ambassador, His Excellency William Van de Weyer, lived at New Lodge, Fifield, Sir Edward Barry (Baron de Barry of Portugal), High Sheriff of Berkshire, lived at Ockwells. The Oppenheimers were at White Waltham and another diamond man, Arnold Litkie, one of the early pioneers of the African fields, lived at Clarefield, Pinkneys Green.

Carlton Mead, the Victorian fiction writer, was in fact William Eglington of Raylands. He once owned both the New Age and the Tatler. He also had interests in diamonds. Today, Eric Bruton edits a national jewellery magazine, writes on horology, and crime novels, and runs two Maidenhead shops, one the Diamond Boutique.

Even the town's architects included extraordinary men. Edward Arnold Radclyffe of

Brookmead, Bray was one of the best known art critics and connoisseurs of his day, and Henry Stanton Webber, son of the High Street shop-keeper, became advising engineer to the military governor of Pretoria. His office was at 47 Queen Street.

Lord Boston, lord-in-waiting to Queen Victoria, lived at Hedsor, and Mr Spencer, father of Stanley of Cookham, attended the house to give piano lessons. Emile Garke of Ditton House, founded the British Electric Traction Company and launched Garke's Electrical Manual and later the Electrical Press in Maidenhead. After the Pococks, Ray Lodge became the home of William Lassall who made many discoveries from his observatory there and ranked with Herschell. He became president of the Royal Astronomical Society in 1870.

Thus the great and medium families formed a periphery of sparkle round the town, but there were two families who lit up the entire horizon—the Grenfells and the Astors. The Grenfells came from Marazion, Cornwall. Pascoe Grenfell (1729-1810) was in the tin and copper ore business in a big way in the City. His son, Pascoe Grenfell (1761-1838) became the head of this concern. He bought Taplow Court from the Earl of Orkney and became MP for Great Marlow (1802-1820). The property passed to William Henry Grenfell, who became Lord Desborough in 1905. Mr Grenfell married Ethel Anne Fane, only daughter of the Hon Julian Fane. They had five children. Julian and Gerald were killed in France in 1915, Ivo was killed in a motor accident in 1926, Monica married Marshall of the RAF Sir John Salmon, and Imogen married Viscount Gage.

Lord Desborough became the man of his century. President Taft was once asked, 'Who typifies the English gentleman?'. He replied, 'Lord Desborough'. Desborough stroked an eight across the Channel and was the only man to row in the Grand Challenge at Henley Royal while an MP. He swam across Niagara Falls pool twice, sculled a crew of three with a 12st cox from London to Oxford in 22 hours non-stop, was Thames punting champion for three years, fenced for England and won the Epee Prize for three years in succession at the Royal Military Tournament, climbed the Matterhorn by three different routes, hunted big game in the Rockies, India and Africa, and caught 100 tarpen off Florida.

He organised the 1908 Olympic Games, was a Knight of the Garter, Captain of the Yeomen of the Guard, Chairman of the Thames Conservancy for 32 years, twice mayor of Maidenhead and its High Steward for 60 years.

The Port of London Act was due to his energies and he was largely responsible for the reform of Police pay and conditions. He framed a scheme for the reform of the House of Lords. He presided over the MCC, the Lawn Tennis Association, the Amateur Fencing Association, Four-in-hand Driving Club, Coaching Club, London Chamber of Commerce, British Dairy Farmers Association, and the Shorthorn Society. He also farmed. His Betty Denton was female champion all breeds at the 1932 Royal Show.

He found time to write many books on travel, and was a war correspondent for the Daily Telegraph in the Sukin Campaign when he was chased by Dervishes. They were not to know that he was an Oxford three-miler. He outpaced them.

Desborough turned down the governor-generalship of Canada in 1921, but they did name an avenue after him in Alberta, and in 1917 the Great Western Railway christened one of their locomotives Taplow Court.

His small daughter Monica once asked him, 'Can God make such a tall man as you, why you are taller than Mrs Neave (cook at Taplow for 31 years) and the kitchenmaid'. He was a tall man in any company.

Royalty were frequent visitors at Taplow Court. Lady Desborough's published papers carry this note: 'The King and Queen and all their children came over to Taplow at the end of their holidays'. Along Thames-side one could have watched Lord Kitchener baiting the hooks for the young Grenfells. His biographer, Sir George Arthur, said that Desborough was almost the only man in the world in whom Kitchener had implicit trust. He always spent the first week of his leave at Taplow. Desborough died in 1945 at 89, his wife in 1952 at 84. The family's Maidenhead estates covered 12,000 acres.

Cliveden became the country seat of the Astors, the family that owned New York. The original house was built by the notorious George Villiers, Duke of Buckingham. His duel with the Earl of Shrewsbury is commemorated by Pope's contemptuous lines:

Gallant and gay in Cliveden's proud alcove
The bower of wanton Shrewsbury and love

Her husband mortally wounded, Buckingham 'slept with her that night in his bloody shirt.'

The second Viscount Astor followed Lord Desborough as High Steward. In 1873 his father bought Cliveden from the Duke of Westminster. Like Pascoe Grenfell, Mr Astor did things in a big way. He bought the massive stone balustrade, 200 yards long, from the Villa Borghese and transported it to Cliveden. He bought the Observer, the Pall Mall Gazette, and a vast quantity of art treasures. In 1906, when his son married Nancy Langhorne of Virginia, he gave Cliveden to him as a wedding present. The second Viscount set up the famous Cliveden Stud. It won more than 460 races and was placed in 547 others. One win was the Royal Hunt Cup at Ascot in 1926. The cup is part of the town's collection of silver plate. He built Cliveden Hospital and gave it to the Canadian Army, and finally gave Cliveden to the National Trust. He wrote of Cliveden: 'My wife and I have tried to use it to bring about a better understanding between the English speaking world and between various groups and sections of people in this and other countries'. He hoped that Cliveden would continue to be so used. The present occupants are Stanford University of California.

The first Lord Astor is buried in the chapel which stands at the edge of the cliff overlooking the Thames. It is resplendent in gold mosaics. He converted it from a gazebo built by Giacomo for the first Lord Orkney in 1735.

Both Desborough and Astor were involved with Maidenhead Cottage Hospital, but its arrival was largely due to John Hibbert of Braywick Lodge (1811-1888). He had helped to establish Windsor Hospital of which he became a chief benefactor. He also built St Mark's Church, now attached to the geriatric unit at St Mark's Hospital. His beautifully landscaped grounds are a public park.

But it was the Pearce family who knitted old Maidenhead into modern times. They lived at the Manor House. All that remains to mark its garden are the yew trees in the middle of the Castle Hill roundabout. Kidwells Park was its grounds and Pelham Court in Marlow Road stands on part of its farm. J. D. M. Pearce, son of a congregational minister, was mayor five times between 1856-1890. His son, Major J. E. Pearce, introduced electricity to Maidenhead in 1902. As a consultant he had been responsible for the building of Galway Power Station, and had invented many of the devices in common use in power stations in his day. He built the town's first concrete houses, (now covered by Evenlode), was a horologist, and one of the first motorists in town, driving a 24hp Argyll. His large property interests—the Craufurd Estate—comprised 210 freehold houses, shops and business premises. He was Mayor in 1902. He lived at Craufurd Hall, which he turned into the town's first all-electric house with its own generator and the newest kitchen novelty—an electric cooker. Thus the Pearce family bridged the years to modern Maidenhead.

ABOVE LEFT: Arms of the Pocock family.

ABOVE RIGHT: Sir Thomas Bodley.

CENTRE: George Villiers, Duke of Buckingham.
(The Mansell Collection).

BELOW: Spencer Gallery, Cookham.

80

ABOVE LEFT: Sir Stanley Spencer.

ABOVE RIGHT: Frederick Lewis, Prince of Wales.
(The Mansell Collection).

CENTRE: The Duchess of Sutherland.
(The Mansell Collection).

BELOW: Sir George Young's house with Cliveden woods.

81

ABOVE: Cliveden House: the gazebo (left) became a chapel
thanks to the first Viscount Astor.

BELOW: Hedsor Lodge at harvest time.

82

ABOVE LEFT: Taplow Court.

RIGHT: Nancy, Lady Astor.

Cliveden Spring—site of a cottage in the news in the sixties.

The leading front page—the first Advertiser.

ABOVE LEFT: Frederick George Baylis, virtual founder, who took the Advertiser over in 1872.

ABOVE RIGHT: Philip Thompson, once manager of Skindles.

BELOW LEFT: Louis G. Baylis, founder of the modern Advertiser.

BELOW RIGHT: Ernest Dunkels of Woodhurst, Ray Mead road, a quiet benefactor.

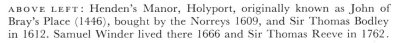

ABOVE LEFT: Henden's Manor, Holyport, originally known as John of Bray's Place (1446), bought by the Norreys 1609, and Sir Thomas Bodley in 1612. Samuel Winder lived there 1666 and Sir Thomas Reeve in 1762.

BELOW LEFT: Sir Edward Barry, High Sheriff of Berkshire, 1907/8, of Ockwells Manor.

ABOVE RIGHT: Lord Boston of Hedsor Wharf.

CENTRE RIGHT: Lord Desborough, as a younger man.

BELOW RIGHT: Sir Henry Vansittart Neale of Bisham Abbey.

86

ABOVE LEFT: Abraham Hoffnung of Rawdon Hall, Holyport.

BELOW LEFT: R. C. Lehmann, editor of the Daily News in 1901.

ABOVE RIGHT: Col F. C. Ricardo, Lullebrook Manor, Cookham.

CENTRE: Ditton House, built 1865, home of Emile Garcke;
on the site of a 14th century house.

BELOW RIGHT: James Drummond, proprietor St Ives Hotel.

ABOVE LEFT: William Eglington, otherwise Carlton Meade.

CENTRE: James Rutland of Ye Gables, Taplow, and Taeppa's discoverer.

BELOW LEFT: E. J. Shrewsbury, architect.

ABOVE RIGHT: H. Stanton Webber.

BELOW RIGHT: Valerian Arnold Litkie, diamond man.

High Street Story

Victorian tradesmen pioneered the town as a business centre, providing its mayors and councillors, and making it into a self-sufficient place. They offered shopping with dignity and drawing-room manners. Their showcases displayed the prosperity of the Empire and the wealthy were enticed from their big houses to shop by flattery through superb service. They invented a High Street culture in shop-keeping. It was a glorious era of private trading in which the customer was always right. It blossomed and died.

The last of the quality shops to bow out, having sunk so low as to offer goods on hire purchase, was Biggs. Queen Mary shopped there in its Bond Street atmosphere making six successive annual expeditions. To be seen in High Street carrying a parcel gift-wrapped in Biggs's black and gold paper, singled you out as a person appreciative of the best.

The Victorian age was a time of master and servant, of maids and mistresses, and rough times for the poorly off. There were long hours for shop assistants whose rights were secondary to those of their masters and customers. There were echelons of shopping and the lower orders shopped in the lower echelons. A customer entering a shop above her station could be frozen in her tracks by a glance from a properly trained shop walker. Those high priests who walked the aisles of drapers' shops could spot a feather hat made by a plumassier at a hundred yards.

But the goods they sold were made to last—even suits. Never Never Dunn, one time proprietor of James Moores, the town's oldest outfitters, made a suit for Ned Cooper, Lord Astor's head game-keeper, which he reputedly wore for 40 years.

High Street characters who gave such diversity of interest to the street, extended from Quaker Rous, an outfitter, to Phil Thompson, the grocer who managed Skindles Hotel, rode to the Queen's Royal Buckhounds, and drove a four-wheeled American style buggy from Maidenhead, round Piccadilly Circus and into Hyde Park. They included Fredrick Parker Such, who had descended from the Hanoverian courtiers De Sach. His family came to England with George I. All of them became deeply involved in the town that they were building, in its amateur club life of regattas, cricket, football and histrionics. They acted, sang, preached, marketed, and mongered and held their heads high. Success was a frock coat and a house on Castle Hill Estate, coupled, if possible, with a mayoral chain. Many achieved it, and a seat on the aldermanic bench. Some became known abroad. Mr Burnham, a printer and stationer, was decorated by the Belgian and French Fire Brigades, and was Fire Brigades Staff Officer for the Lord Mayor's Show. A boiling wake of nostalgia for the good old days of Maidenhead followed their passing. The marketing men and salesmen came with their certificates of proficiency into this arena of the great amateurs and swept every vestige of individuality from High Street. Though some sham names remained on shop fronts, the counting houses were filled with strangers. Old Maidenhead died and the town lost its way in a welter of supermarkets.

In early times, tradesmen had to be admitted freemen of the town before they could carry on their trade. On August 28, 1676, one who wished to be admitted a freeman and exercise his trade as a tailor, had to attend the Town Hall for an interview with the Mayor, Warden and burgesses. They passed him, and he paid over £5 admission fee to the Bridge-master. At the other end of the scale, on December 31, 1746, Henry Youse became apprenticed to his blacksmith uncle, Robert Youse of Braywick, for seven years, starting as a blower boy. The said Robert 'in consideration for his natural love and affection for his nephew, and in consideration of five shillings in lawful money of Great Britain, to him in hand paid by James Youse', agreed. He also agreed to provide young Henry with meat, drink, washing, lodging, linen, woollen stockings, and shoes as often as need be during his apprenticeship.

By 1760 there were 80 traders using scales, weights, and measures in High Street. Among them were 10 publicans on the Bray side, a cider maker (presumably from nearby apple orchards), a tallow chandler, two collar makers (probably for horses and ponies), a sack weaver, a fellmonger (dealer in skins), one tripe woman, a draper, six farmers and gardeners, and three general shop-keepers. Farms touched the street and part of it was in the shade of fruit trees. Some of the last of the Orchard trees still bloom in Courtlands. Victorian children played on the town green, which was a piece of open land between Broadway and the house of a Mr Kingston, a Thames barge owner, and now the Advertiser office. Travelling showmen were still setting up their stands there in the late 19th century. It was this place which the Victorians transformed.

The first sounds of industry began at the foot of Castle Hill. On dark evenings showers of sparks and flames rose above the roof of Mr Rodgers' iron foundry, between High and West Streets. One of the most important engineering firms in the county was to grow out of this foundry—Battings. Nearby, Tom Lamb could be heard cutting blocks of stone in his mason's yard. Today, Lamb & Co is in All Saints Avenue. But the most influential man of all came from Buckingham.

Reared in an atmosphere of brewing and religious piety he grew restless in the family home and bought No. 63 High Street in 1766. He was James Stuchbery. His brother Thomas, master brewer of Buckingham, was part of the Stuchbery brewing empire of that town and county. A couple of years later, the Silver family, builders, moved to Bray. They can trace their family history to the 1500s. By 1818 Richard Silver had established Altwood works at Tittle Row and shortly afterwards opened an office and joiners' business in High Street, employing highly-skilled stone masons. Another young man, Robert Nicholson, a grocer from Lincoln, came to town to take a job with Stuchbery's. He afterwards bought No. 53 and set up a general provisions store. The Stuchberys, Silvers, and Nicholsons became the formidable advance guard for the High Street pioneers. As the town grew, their influence, talents, and benevolence helped to shape and direct it.

James Stuchbery was joined by his nephew Tom in 1802, an extremely competent businessman, who brought with him the evangelical fervour of the Buckinghamshire brewers. He taught young Nicholson the art of the brewmaster. Robert Nicholson began brewing at the back of his new shop, trundling the beer round town on a hand cart. It was his eldest son William Nicholson, born 1820, who started the Pineapple Brewery in Maidenhead High Street, probably so called because the first pineapple in England was grown at Dorney Court by a man called Rose, gardener to the Palmer family. The Pineapple public house at Dorney is a memorial to this historic piece of horticulture.

Beer and religion were also mixed by the Langton family, whose brewery was in East and Market Streets (Isaacs Stores). They worshipped at the Congregational Church, West Street and provided mugs of beer for Sunday school scholars on special occasions.

Another early shop keeper whose family business began in the 1790s, and who was eventually taken over by W. H. Smith & Sons, was William Burnham. He had various High Street addresses, including 55 and 57, and opened the town's first lending library. He had a print shop in Bell Street. His son James was the fireman, Captain of the Borough Fire Brigade and secretary of Maidenhead Regatta for 14 years.

The second wave of big names came about mid-century. They included Hamblett the sporting fishmonger, the Carters who are still in business in King Street, E. T. Biggs, Julius Neve, and the impeccable James Courtis Webber.

The old White Hart Inn, the remains of which were demolished for the Precinct entrance, was geographically and socially the centre of the town. Fifty horses and a score of coaches used to be stabled there. It became the booking office for the Victoria, Maidenhead, Windsor, and South Western Omnibus Co., headquarters of the collector of taxes, home of the first fire engine, and its telephone number was Maidenhead one. Nicholson's Brewery was established on the site of its stables and coach house.

It was to the White Hart that William Hamblett went to put up his pony when he came into town. He fell in love with the barmaid and married her. Mr and Mrs Hamblett took over No. 80. There, Mrs Hamblett in black dress and white apron, dispensed fish, shrimps, and winkles. Business flourished. William installed the first marble slabs in town for displaying his fish. Previously they were of slate. In the 1870s he built the mammoth Hamblettonian Hall in Market Street. Its size was not to be surpassed until the Leisure Centre went up nearby in 1975. He surrounded the building with trees and gardens. The floor for roller skating swept out of the hall, passed round the gardens, and re-entered the hall by another door. The building still stands as Mead's Garage, now owned by Lex. A large outdoor swimming pool was opened on adjoining land in 1876, when, with a show of ostentation to match the occasion the mayor threw a glass of champagne into the water to christen it. Some of the first water pumped by the new Maidenhead Water Co. filled the pool. It was later called the Grand Hall. Philharmonic orchestras, Susa's Band, and theatricals played there. There were indoor circuses, Victorian soirées, and David Lloyd George to address a political meeting. The whole flamboyant enterprise failed. It was too ambitious for the size of the town. It was also freezing cold in winter through inadequate heating arrangements. Hamblett the fishmonger, as distinct from Hamblett the impresario, used to cut ice in winter for his fish shop from the Moor stream. He stored it in the ice wells and bank at Castle Hill. Ice wells were fairly common on big estates, and these were thought to have been used originally by the old Sun Inn. They were England's first deep freezers. When Hamblett died, his widow built a house over the old wells which came to be known as the Ice House. It still stands.

Today, Mr and Mrs George Carter, saddlers, of King Street, run one of the town's few quality shops, based on leather craftsmanship. It began more than a century ago in High Street when teams of yoked oxen would stop outside for harness repairs. Another well-known family set up shop at No. 59 in 1847, led by Julius Neve, a fervent Baptist. It survived as a men's outfitters for more than 120 years, ending at No. 74, having descended to Alderman John Neve, who was mayor in 1969 as his father was in 1941 and 1942. But of all the personalities of Victorian Maidenhead, the influence of one—James Courtis

Webber—was projected into the 20th century. His ghost must have walked the store, for the reputation which was built into this business refused to die until eventually the store became part of a chain and the Webber touch was lost. About 1856 he opened at No. 64 a little shop that customers stepped down to. He built it up into a department store, and handed the ladies out of their carriages when they came to shop. Eventually it had apprentices' bedrooms on the top floor, a restaurant and 400 to watch its fashion parades. Later, McIlroys and Butler's Stores, joined Webber's to make three department stores along High Street. Mid-century also, Spindlers the bakers arrived, as did Heybournes, who were to sell the first motor car here but began in chinaware, and from Kensington came John Budgen.

Maidenhead owes some homage to all these families because they made the town their business. Most of those families are still here. There also arrived, from Gloucestershire, a young journalist, Fredrick Baylis, who took over the recently founded Maidenhead Advertiser from a local syndicate. His grandson, Louis Baylis, virtually gave the newspaper to Maidenhead in 1962, when he set up the Louis Baylis (Maidenhead Advertiser) Charitable Trust in 1962. He was another great Maidonian.

How Stuchbery's the grocers became Stuchbery's the lawyers is perhaps High Street's most remarkable family story. It centres around Jane Thompson, who came from a well-known Wargrave family who had been cheese factors in Reading for many years—a remarkable woman who was to play a leading part in the town's business life after she became Mrs Owen Stuchbery.

The four firms of Stuchbery, Nicholson, Webber, and Budgen came to dominate the street.

Robert Nicholson's grocery and provision business developed into a prosperous concern. He also became a candlemaker, using fat from local butchers. He made 'tenners' and 'eighteens' (burning time). He set up a bacon factory at the back of his shop and pigs were driven along Brock Lane to slaughter, the trotters being thrown over the wall into the lane where they were scrambled for by small boys. Not everyone was rich. The business was developed by his grandson. Both men reached the mayoralty.

It was old Robert's son William who founded the brewery in 1840. It was a small red-bricked square building with louvred ventilators for the coolers. It stood at the bottom of Nicholson's Lane, a rural approach from the then Braywick Road. To the south were the gardens of Queen Street traders, an orchard, in the middle of which was Master Pert the Cobbler's cottage, and the gardens of the White Hart. The smell of fresh grains and hops wafted into High Street as they were turned out from the mash tuns into farmers' carts. Mr Nicholson walked to the brewery at 5.30 am every morning carrying a lantern and an umbrella. As the swinging light was spotted, the first man in the messroom would have the master's glass ready by the time he arrived. The 14 employees were allowed a tallboy of beer four times a day. In addition to brewing, Mr Nicholson, not unlike the great W. G. Grace in appearance, played cricket. He was a member of the Maidenhead team of 18, who in 1835, beat an all-England team in the town. The club originated in the 1770s, playing the first cricket in the county. His last game, when he was over 80, was for the Corporation. He supplied the horses that pulled the cricket club's roller. Eventually a house for Mr Nicholson, and a brewery office were built on an extensive High Street frontage. The firm became a private company in 1903 and eventually had 150 tied houses. Courages bought it and the shopping precinct stands upon it. One of the last beers to be brewed there had a jaunty Maidenhead name—Double Nick.

Stuchberys, meanwhile, were expanding in spite of old Tom's sermons. He was a friend of the Countess of Huntingdon, the noted non-conformist and had built a chapel among his store sheds at the bottom of White Hart Lane. He had looked after his family well, having provided houses for them at Hill Cottage, Cromwell Cottage (the title deed goes back to Elizabeth I) and Berry Villa, all on the Bath Road. In 1891, his second son, Richard, landscaped Grenfell Park, (which his friend, Mr Grenfell had given to the town), built the lodge, and put the iron railings round it. The family line descends through the third son William Owen (born 1823). He married Jane Thompson, who ran the administrative side of this expanding business. Calamity came for Jane when Owen died at 46. Old Tom, who had never forgiven his son for marrying her, redrafted his will so that the business should be sold over her head. She received nothing. But Jane was a remarkable woman. With the aid of her family she bought the business back, made it into an emporium and traded under the name of Stuchbery and Thompson. In 1883 she married Alderman Richard Silver, the successful builder, and they went to live at The Firs, Castle Hill. There were so many visitors and relatives dropping in for the week-end that Richard decided to build another house in the orchard. While digging in the garden he came across the remains of a Roman villa.

Jane settled her interests in the stores on her three children, and remembering her own legal battle was determined to have a lawyer in the family. Thomas William Stuchbery, her only son, qualified with honours in 1889, and that was how the legal firm of Park Street began. At Stuchbery & Thompson there was an apprentice whose name at the time was not important. He was Walter Court from Canterbury. His family are back in town. Their furniture business is at the corner of St Ives Road.

In 1876, 30-year-old John Budgen, whose family had a provisions business in Kensington, bought Nicholson's grocery business and in 1881 the adjoining property and added an ironmongery department. The tallow factory continued and he even exported to Germany. John Budgen pronounced for progress and the public good and was soon on his way to the mayoral chair.

Nos. 49 and 51 were previously occupied by a nurseryman named Elliott who invented Summer Cloud, the green shade paint still put on glasshouses in summer. Mr Budgen re-built the entire block 49-55. He opened many branches and the business is now a well-known chain.

The International Stores took over the Stuchbery business, and in 1922 Sydney R. Thompson, who became chairman of the Borough Bench, took over the ironmongery section of Budgens (now Freeman Hardy & Willis). Eventually an expanding Webbers took over Thompsons. They also took over S. R. Hermon of Grenfell Road who made some of the first wireless sets in town, sold by Webbers under the trade name Webberphone. These shops provided the main support services for a self-contained community. They made, mended, and mixed. Stuchbery's tin and copper smiths made servants' trunks and cooking utensils for riverside hotels. Paint mixers produced individual orders. No one carried shopping. The delivery service was exemplary. As it turned out T. W. Stuchbery the lawyer outshone all the tradesmen in public service. He was the last feudal mayor, reaching the chair five times. Remarkably, he was also clerk to the rural authority, coroner, superintendent registrar, secretary of the Waterworks Company, chairman of the electricity undertaking, and attained high office in Freemasonry. No wonder the police held up the traffic when they heard him approaching the town on his large motor cycle, a machine which some said he never mastered, although he was one of the first people here to ride one.

Mr Rogers' foundry at the bottom of Castle Hill was bought by Battings of Marlow in 1872. Mr Rogers then set up the town's first steam laundry at Furze Platt, now Clean. Battings moved to 134 High Street, bought a large site behind it in West Street and built there the most up-to-date foundry and engineering works in the county. When the GWR was extended from Taplow to Twyford, Charles Batting's firm built the eleven road bridges, including Braywick and Forlease arches, and two footbridges. After use as Webbers' furniture depository, Post Office Telephones took that over. Originally it was part of the garden of the old Greyhound Inn.

The man who left his mark on lower High Street was George Gude. An artist and photographer, he came from Hackney, about 1890, to set up a photographer's business at No. 7. He had sittings with King Edward VII, Madame Melba and other notables such as the Portuguese Ambassador and Lord Curzon, during their visits to the town. Opposite his shop abutting Chapel Arches there was a piece of open land. He built the Hippodrome there and surrounded it with ornamental gardens. The Colonnade now stands on it. Lady Desborough performed the opening ceremony for his roller skating rink, which is currently doing duty as a factory. His daughter is Mrs Margaret Pitcher, who this year was made an MBE by the Queen for her public service to Maidenhead through the King George VI Club and the Women's Voluntary Service.

Outside High Street, apart from a ring of breweries and chapels, a number of people were at work on the town's character. Among them was Fredrick Parker Such. He made an academic start at 45 Bridge Road by opening a dairy with a school room at the back where the Misses Such set up Such's Academy. They later founded Elmslie School on Castle Hill. Behind was an orchard and Mr Such moved into the market garden business. His son founded the Royal Berkshire Nursery in Braywick Road and in about 1877 took over Boyn Hill Farm which then stretched to Grenfell Road with a farmhouse where the East Berks College is, and opened a dairy at 78 Queen Street. In 1880, he sold the farm to Edward Brill who specialised in growing strawberries there until Clare and Laburnham Roads were built upon it. In 1887 he was joined by Daniel Herbert Brown from Perthshire, who married Clara Such.

The Braywick Road nursery of about 100 acres stretched to Stafferton Lodge—the rise in the road used to be known as Such's Hill. The firm of Brown & Such became famous and naturally opened a shop in High Street. Mr Brown began exhibiting dahlias at the Crystal Palace in 1889. His wife and his son John were to make them famous all over the world as the business won international fame. John Brown's nursery, like Brills strawberry beds, eventually disappeared under housing—Greenfields. A roundabout stands where his greenhouses abutted Braywick Road. But John Brown is still the president of the National Dahlia Society and a Chelsea Show judge. Another famous plant raiser was Mr Simkin, the workhouse master. He raised the Mrs Simkin pink when workhouse master at Slough.

To get the town moving in a more interesting way Mr H. J. Timberlake established a cycle works in Queen Street in the 1860s and began building velocipedes. The first issue of the Advertiser, July 28, 1869, reported Mr Timberlake's race challenge to Mr Louis Rumball, an athlete who had won the mile-and-a-half steeplechase cup at Chertsey. The stakes were £10 a side and a silver tankard to the winner. An immense crowd including the neighbouring gentry assembled to witness the event over a mile course on the Thicket. Thirty yards from the start Timberlake crashed. He injured both himself and Rumball the runner. Gipsies were blamed for the accident and Rumball collected the prize. Timber-lakes flourished down the years as did Hickling & Co., whose Pilot Cycle Works took over Hamblett's Hall and turned it into a cycle factory. The hall began its service to the new motor industry at A. W. Heybourne & Company's Grand Garage. Eventually it became R. S. Mead's garage, specialising in Rolls Royces. Mr Reggie Mead who lives at Winter Hill, also opened a garage at Tittle Row. Richard Silver was his ancestor, which is where we came in. It's a small world in a small town.

ABOVE : Chapel Arches.

BELOW LEFT : Biggs, the jewellers.

BELOW RIGHT : Battings.

ABOVE: left to right—William Owen Stuchbery, Richard Silver and
Jane Thompson (Tom Stuchbery).

BELOW: John Clare, No 2 drayman for Nicholson's, covered
Twyford, Wargrave and Henley.

96

ABOVE : Langton's Brewery, West street.

CENTRE LEFT : Old Maltings, School lane, Cookham.
(Drawn by Amy Hagerty Spencer).

BELOW LEFT : Pineapple (Nicholson's) Brewery.

BELOW RIGHT : Pineapple Brewery label 1878/1901.

97

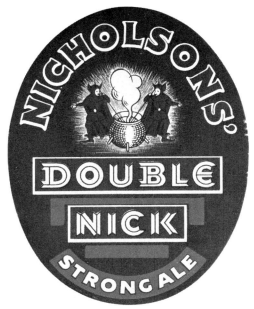

LEFT: Nicholson's Brewery—made way for the precinct.

ABOVE RIGHT: Double Nick—Nicholson's last new beer.

BELOW RIGHT: Saddler George Carter at work.

ABOVE: Stuchbery's Stores staff outing.

BELOW: Station Approach, 1904.

99

ABOVE : Hamblettonian Hall.

BELOW : Queen Anne Hotel, Castle Hill—built by Cooper's as a living
showcase of their wide variety of decorative brickwork.

ABOVE LEFT: John Budgen, Mayor 1895.

ABOVE RIGHT: Shirley, Castle Hill—John Budgen's home.

CENTRE LEFT: Manor House, Marlow road, Maidenhead, now gone—once the oldest house in the town.

BELOW LEFT: Eric F. Such.

CENTRE RIGHT: Herbert Brown.

BELOW RIGHT: W. Burnham.

101

R. H. Sands & Sons, the Queen street furnishers, as it was in 1908.
Today's modern business is still in the family, run by Mr P. J. Sands of the
third generation.

ABOVE LEFT: Charles Batting.

ABOVE RIGHT: T. W. Stuchbery, last feudal Mayor.

BELOW: Crauford College, Gringer Hill, demolished 1949.

ABOVE LEFT: Mr Cumings of the station yard made landaus like this one he advertised in 1890's.

ABOVE RIGHT: Timberlake's Cycle Factory.

CENTRE: Landau in Queen street.

BELOW: Taxi! Station Approach.

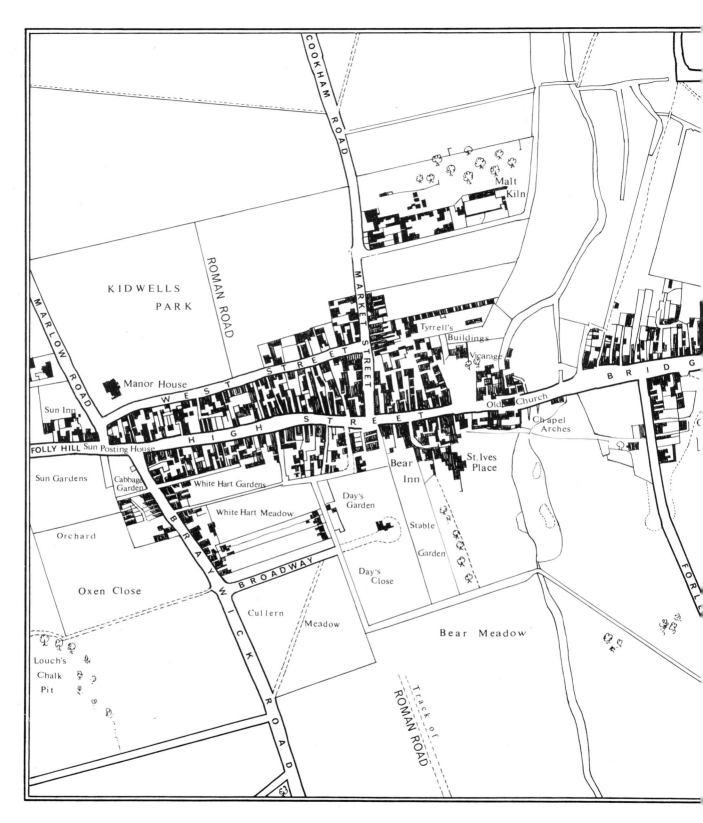

Alderman Silver's 1907 drawing of an 1830 map of Maidenhead town centre—redrawn in 1975 for this book by Tony Pickford.

104

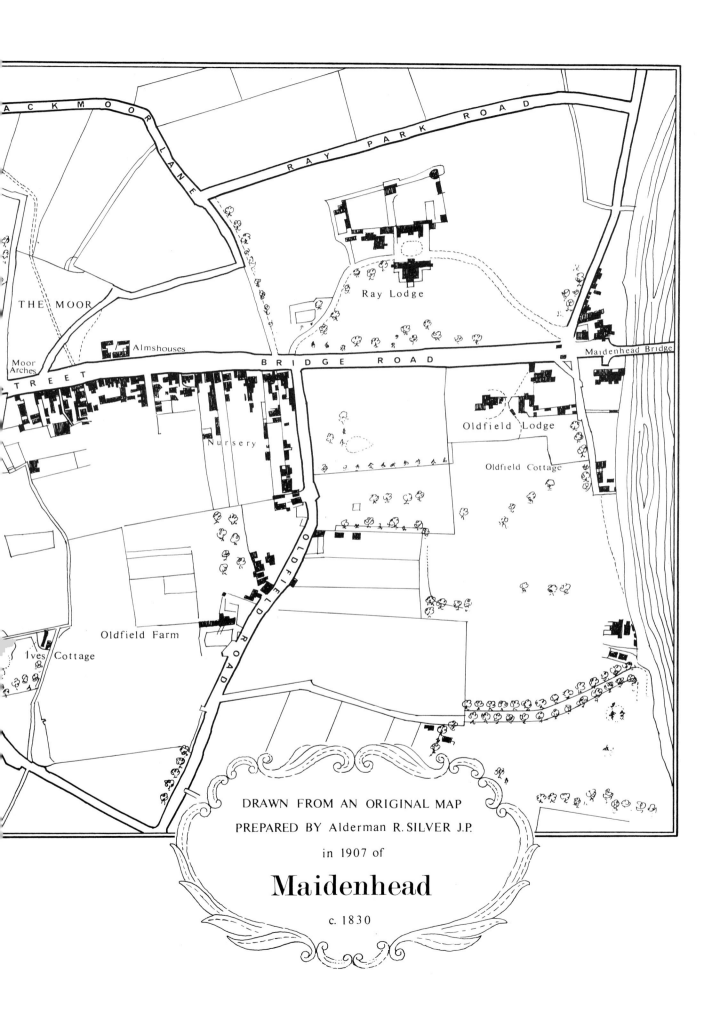

DRAWN FROM AN ORIGINAL MAP

PREPARED BY Alderman R. SILVER J.P.

in 1907 of

Maidenhead

c. 1830

The Maidenhead Steam Laundry,

MOSSY HILL, MAIDENHEAD.

Every Convenience for executing Large or Small Quantities of Work. CAREFULNESS, Good Work, and Prompt Delivery we make a particular study.

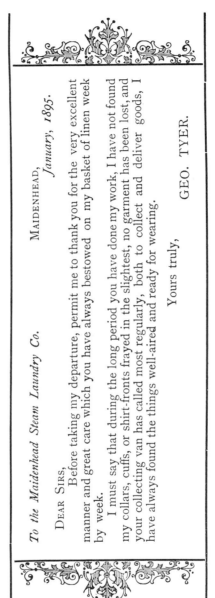

To the Maidenhead Steam Laundry Co.

MAIDENHEAD,
January, 1895.

DEAR SIRS,

Before taking my departure, permit me to thank you for the very excellent manner and great care which you have always bestowed on my basket of linen week by week.

I must say that during the long period you have done my work, I have not found my collars, cuffs, or shirt-fronts frayed in the slightest, no garment has been lost, and your collecting van has called most regularly, both to collect and deliver goods, I have always found the things well-aired and ready for wearing.

Yours truly, GEO. TYER.

Special Terms are offered to Schools, Hotels, Clubs, &c. Address—MANAGER or MANAGERESS,

MAIDENHEAD STEAM LAUNDRY,

MOSSY HILL, MAIDENHEAD.

VANS AND CARTS TO ALL PARTS DAILY.

Maidenhead Steam Laundry advertisement, 1890's.

ABOVE LEFT : Castle Hill and the Ice House.

ABOVE RIGHT : Clock Tower, and Temperance Hotel.

CENTRE : Kidwells Park entry pre-relief road.   RIGHT : The Colonnade.

BELOW LEFT : Chapel Arches 1895.

107

ABOVE: Workers at James Hews, plumbers of 69 High street.

BELOW: Milkmen in Queen street.

108

MAIDENHEAD
Permanent Benefit Building and Investment Society.

Register No. *35*

This is to Certify, that *Julius Nive*
of *Maidenhead* became
a Member of the above Society on the *fourth*
of *April* 18 *59* and is the holder of *five*
Share.
Dated *6th* day of *April* 18 *59*

Brown Secretary.

ABOVE: H. W. Woodhouse's Bridge street business.

GRAND AEROSTATIC FETE
AT
MAIDENHEAD.

Balloon Ascent,

Under the patronage of the Worshipful the Mayor, and the leading Gentry of Maidenhead and its Vicinity.

Mr. C. GREEN
Aéronaut to the
ROYAL GARDENS, VAUXHALL,
And Proprietor of
GREAT NASSAU BALLOON
With which he performed the memorable Continental Trip
FROM LONDON TO NASSAU IN GERMANY,
A Distance of
580 MILES in 18 HOURS.
Respectfully announces to the Inhabitants and Visitors of Maidenhead and its vicinity, that he purposes making his 402nd, Ascent
On TUESDAY, AUGUST 1st, 1848,
WITH HIS ROYAL
Victoria Balloon

With which he had the honour to ascend from Cambridge, in the presence of her Majesty his Royal Highness Prince Albert, the Duke of Wellington, Sir Robert Peel, and other distinguished Persons, at His Royal Highness's Installation in July last.

This stupendous Aërostatic Machine is formed with 1,200 yard of Silk, manufactured for the express purpose, in alternate gores of Crimson and Gold, with a Zone or Belt, on which is inscribed "ROYAL VICTORIA," in Gold Letters 3 feet high, with Crowns and other National Emblems. It measures 120 feet in circumference, contains 200,000 gallons of Gas, and with the Car attached is
66 FEET HIGH.
The Ascent will take place from a spacious Meadow belonging to Mr. SPRATLY, Builder,
OPPOSITE MAIDENHEAD MOOR.

A reproduction of the 1848 Balloon Fete programme incorporated in Sunday's programme at White Waltham reported on page 5.

THE "RAY MEAD" HOTEL

LEFT: Up, up and away—in the good old days.

ABOVE RIGHT: H. Hoare, renowned proprietor of Skindles.

CENTRE RIGHT: E. Spindler, pastrycook and confectioner.

BELOW RIGHT: Norkett's dam—at Spencer's Farm, 1913.

110

All That Jazz

Wise men, from the first flint knappers to the frock-coated pillars of Victorian society chose to live on the high ground. They were the prudent people. Their choice of building sites eliminated the risk of property damage through flooding. The more adventurous types lived on the low ground where the highly polished dance floors were. The dancing girls who rode home from theatreland on a train known locally as the Greasepaint Special, dispersed towards the riverside. Inevitably it became a playground area, especially under artificial light, and it was expected of it that it should behave in an extrovert manner. It never let the gossip writers down.

It began with the utmost propriety and discretion. Gentlemen escorting ladies to Murray's Club, where Bridge Gardens is today, wore white ties and tails. The Prince of Wales who became the Duke of Windsor, Carl Brisson, Edgar Wallace, and sundry escorts well-known to first-nighters, could be observed from the dinner tables. As the dance floor was of glass, and illuminated from below, an alternative view could be obtained, after tipping the head waiter, from downstairs. It was an era which followed the official nod for mixed bathing from the aldermanic bench. Mayfair's overspill came first. The reconnaissance parties of playboys formed a bridgehead into Victorian Maidenhead prior to the full invasion by the English after the second world war.

The first sportsmen, of course, were of a different kind. Berkshire cricket began at Old Field in 1773. In 1793, Maidenhead defeated the MCC at Lords. The Daily Chronicle carried the following advertisement:

A Grand Match will be played next Monday in Lords Cricket Ground,
Marybone between nine gentlemen of Marybone Club and two of
Middlesex against eleven of the Maidenhead Club for 500 guineas a side.
The wickets will be pitched at 11 o'clock and the match played out.

The Maidenhead team won.

In 1787, George III and the royal family attended Maidenhead races. More than a century later, in 1871, Maidenhead Football Club, formed in 1869, was one of the original entries in the F.A. Cup, being defeated by Tottenham Hotspurs in the divisional semi-final. In 1853, John Wisden and John Lillywhite were members of a united eleven of England who played Maidenhead at Cricket in Kidwells Park. But national fame came to Maidenhead in 1924, when it became the first upper river club to win the Thames Cup at Henley Royal Regatta. The crew was: H. J. Waizeneker (stroke), R. G. Jackson, H. E. G. Woods, J. G. Barleo, H. J. Fowlie, S. A. Quarterman, R. R. Waterer, W. Boulton, and A. E. Green (cox). John Fowlie became a well-known commentator at Richmond and other horse shows. The outstanding achievement of modern times was performed by John Bushnell and Richard Burnell of Sonning in 1948 when they won a gold medal for their victory in the

Olympic double sculls. In 1935-36 Maidenhead Football Club reached the semi-final of the Amateur Cup.

Artistic people also added to the town's reputation. Well-known actors, artists, writers, and painters have been living here for years, and of course, the excellent hotels brought a discerning custom. The Ray Mead Hotel at Boulters Lock had '30 superb bedrooms, every modern convenience, and illuminated by electric light throughout'. The Old Bell at Hurley, which claims to be the oldest inn in England, originally served the pilgrims visiting the Benedictine settlement there. The Hinds Head Hotel at Bray first served food in the 15th century and was made famous by Barry Neam in the 20th. General Eisenhower dined at the Old Bell during the war and it was there that the distinguished American humorist, James Thurber, wrote the biography of Harold Wallace Ross, founder of the New Yorker Magazine.

Murrays Club was a branch of the London Club. It took over Bridge House, formerly occupied by George Herring, who built the almshouses called the Haven of Rest in 1895. His ashes were buried under the sundial. In the day-time there were fashion parades at Murrays, the models arriving by boat. It was afterwards called the Hungaria. Bridge Gardens covers the spot. There is still fun to be had in style there in the High Steward's Barge. It was brought to Bridge Gardens by John Smith. The Showboat in Oldfield Road, which later became a factory, was another club of the inter-war years.

One of the town's direct links with the stage was through the Two Bobs—Bob Alden and Bob Adams, of Maidenhead. Their big night was when they topped the bill at the Tivoli in 1910; even the orchestra cheered. They had just introduced London to ragtime with Alexander's Ragtime Band. They were two Americans whose names belong to memory-land, but Adams ran Sunny's Club by the riverside for 20 years. It was named after his second wife, a cabaret star called Sunny Brent. He died in 1948, Alden in 1932. Clubland spread along the low ground in the 1920s, largely in the Ray Park area. These night spots were mainly for the tasting of intoxicants. A series of police raids eventually closed those which were not observing the licensing laws. The Ray Park area also provided training quarters for the French heavyweight Georges Carpentier.

Local industry had both a touch of art and a touch of adventure, and the town's traditional link with the stage. Timberlakes, the Queen Street cycle firm, produced the Timberlakes saturator which came to be called lime-light. It was superior to the early floods of that name. Early craftsmen included Barford and Norkett, whose ornamental ironworks in King Street made such meritorious artefacts as cathedral screens for churches here and abroad. S. Evans & Sons took over their premises. Edward Norkett was mayor in 1913 and 1914. He became well-known for his dam. This extraordinary piece of work was built across the narrows in the flood plain at Spencer's Farm. Norkett's Dam was 1,000ft. long, 4ft. high, 3ft. wide at the top, and 15ft. wide at the base. It cost £300.

On December 15, 1914, a big flood was imminent. As water began to show on the Moor the Mayor ordered the sluices closed. The water disappeared. But on January 2, flood water was about to burst over the top of the dam. Mayor Norkett had no option but to draw the sluices. Oldfield and St Mary's wards were inundated. Families took refuge upstairs, some taking pigs and poultry with them. Boats were sunk at Andrews's boathouses.

The industry which brought most colour to the town was motoring. An alderman said it was not the actual harm that they did but the terror that they created. Petrol was 9d a gallon. Three men began the Maidenhead motor industry, which was to have a brief but exciting life. They were Arthur Grice, J. Talfour Wood, and C. M. Keiller. In 1910 they began building a new light car called the GWK at Cordwallis Works and were later joined there by Sir Dennis Burney, designer of the R.101 airship. He began Streamline Cars Ltd. They were of advanced aerodynamic design with straight-eight engines. Then came Capt D. M. K. Marandaz, one of the most romantic personalities in motoring. He and a man called Steelhaft produced the Marseel. It won more than 250 trial awards, and the GWKs had also been winning a share of gold medals. Keiller and Wood had both been apprentices at Swindon where H. F. S. Morgan received his early training. Morgan came to live at Maidenhead and was the last private owner of Canon Hill, Braywick.

Marandaz went on to make Marandaz Specials. He and Mr and Mrs A. E. Moss shared the driving of them in national rallies. Mrs Moss won a first class award in the RAC Rally. Her son Stirling Moss was to have rather bigger successes. Daughter Pat became a well-known horsewoman and rally driver. They lived at Long White Cloud, Bray.

The first car to reach Maidenhead was a 1904 de Dion Boutonville. It arrived in a packing case from France at Mr Albert Heybourne's shop. He used to drive a Marot-Gardon quadricycle. The Anti-Dangerous Motorists' League put up a strong fight (the things frightened the horses) but they lost. After Lady Astor appeared before Mr T. W. Stuchbery and others and was fined £2 for causing an obstruction in High Street and £1 for failing to produce her licence to P-c Sparkes, motoring seemed to become more respectable. Eventually Vandervell Products moved to Maidenhead and Tony Vandervell built the famous Vanwall Special. From 1914 to 1936 more than 1,000 cars were made on the Cordwallis Estate.

Besides the Anti-Dangerous Motorists' League there were other movements afoot to prevent the town plunging further into unvirtuous ways, because even more subtle weapons than motor cars were being used against the solid citizenry. One was jazz and the other the cinema. The outside world was at the town's threshold. A morality campaign was immediately started to put a stop to jazz. This immoral dance was extremely disturbing to Castle Hill Estate. One of the leaders of the campaign was Canon Drummond, vicar of All Saints. He publicly decried the appearance of Busby's Jazz Band at the Town Hall, making his stand at a meeting of the Maidenhead and District Preventative and Rescue Association. The responsibility for starting the cinema rests heavily upon George Gude. In November, 1905 he gave an animated picture show at the Pavilion that he had built at the Colonnade. The films were, A Maiden's Paradise, In a Hurry to Catch a Train, and The Terrible Girls of St Antos. All good degrading stuff. The Picture Theatre, Bridge Road, opened in 1910, on the site of the East Berks Squash Club; the Plaza, Queen Street built by a local syndicate in 1913, and the 1,400 seater Rialto, now the ABC, in 1927.

Maidenhead, however, was to make its own films. Hammer Productions opened Bray Film Studios, and David Hand, who had worked with Disney, moved to Moor Hall, Cookham to set up a cartoon film industry in this country. A number of small companies shot everything from short instructional films to titles for television. Probably the most successful film-making enterprise started at Islet Park with Mr Gerry Anderson and a team of puppeteers. They made a film called Torchy, of which few people have ever heard, but they also made Fireball XL5 and a number of other space age films with puppets and models that are known all over the world. They are currently filming at Bray.

Although the Development Age has changed the appearance of low ground Maidenhead, the artists, writers, actors, and dancers are still here, along with the television personalities who appear on our screens almost every evening. Canon Drummond would be astonished by the turn events have taken.

ABOVE: Lord Desborough stands behind King Edward VII
at one of those Taplow Court parties.

CENTRE: King Teddy takes tea at Monkey Island.

BELOW: Sportsmen of a different class.

TOWN HALL, MAIDENHEAD.

(By Permission of the Worshipful the Mayor, and Uade the Patronage of the elite of the Neighbourhood), the

MAIDENHEAD AMATEUR

EBONY MINSTRELS

HAVE DECIDED ON GIVING THEIR

GRAND EVENING

ENTERTAINMENT

OF REFINED NEGRO MUSIC,

On Thursday, December 18th, 1862,

ASSETED BY

MR. HARRY RICHARDSON,

THE RENOWNED COMIC VOCALIST, FROM THE LONDON THEATRES.

THE MINSTRELS WITH FULL BAND,

Concertina & Violin, 1st & 2nd Banjoes, Drum-Tambourine, & Bones:

New Instruments, New Voices, New Songs, New Incidents of American Negro Character, fully Delineated. Some Soft and Thrillng Music on the first and second Banjoes.

Song. - - "The Country Fair." - - Mr. Richardson,
With Great Variety o Voice and Expression.

Song. - "My own, my guiding Star." - Mr. Bent.

"The Draper's Clerk." A Song of Love and Jealousy.

THE MUSIC LESSON, OR

HAVE YOU SEEN BARLOW.!!

Stump Oration, by Cassebdarius, "Or any other Man."

ADMISSION :—Reserved Seats, 2s; Back Seats, 1s; Children and Schools admitted Half-price, to Front Seats only. Tickets may be obtained at Mr. Burnham's, High Street, Maidenhead.

DOORS OPEN AT HALF-PAST SEVEN, TO COMMENCE AT EIGHT O'CLOCK PRECISELY.
CARRIAGES ORDERED AT TEN O'CLOCK.

W. BURNHAM, PRINTER, HIGH STREET, MAIDENHEAD.

Playbill—19th century style.

ABOVE LEFT: Off to Ascot Races.

CENTRE LEFT: Four-in-hand awaits custom at The Bear.

BELOW LEFT: Ivy-clad Skindles.

RIGHT: Horton Grange, Raymead road—home of
Henry Seebohm, ornithologist.

116

ABOVE: Roller hockey quintet
BELOW: The Pavilion Cadets.

117

Maidenhead Roller Skating Rink,
PAVILION GARDENS.

PROPRIETOR - - - Mr. GEO. GUDE.

Invitation
To view the OPENING of the New Rink
BY
The Rt. Hon. the Lord Desborough, K.C.V.O.,
WHO WILL BE ACCOMPANIED BY
THE LADY DESBOROUGH,
ON
...NDAY, February 28th, 1910, at 4 p.m.

ABOVE LEFT: Maidenhead Norfolkians FC 1904/5.

CENTRE LEFT: Maidenhead FC 1911/12.

BELOW LEFT: Invitation to the opening of
Mr Gude's Pavilion skating rink.

RIGHT: Royal Hunt Cup—won by Astor in 1926,
through the Cliveden Stud.

118

ABOVE LEFT : Skating interior.

CENTRE LEFT : What's on.

ABOVE RIGHT : The rink.

CENTRE RIGHT : Playspot in Oldfield road—The Showboat.

BELOW : Early motorists at the Tollhouse.

ABOVE : Old timers on parade.

CENTRE : Putting on the style.

BELOW : End of a lovely day.

ABOVE: Two seater 10.8 hp GWK, 1922/23 made at Cordwallis estate.

BELOW: Marandaz Special 15/90, built for road trials, driven by
Mrs A. E. Moss, mother of Stirling. (Beaulieu Motor Museum).

121

ABOVE: Marandaz Motor Works (1934).

BELOW: Golden Cockerel Press—a works of a different kind, at Waltham
St Lawrence—where fine editions were lovingly produced (Richard Gibbs).

ABOVE: Maidenhead Thicket Bowling Club.

BELOW LEFT: Destination: Windsor, Ascot—and the open road.

BELOW RIGHT: Bert Bushnell, Olympic Double Sculls gold medallist 1948.

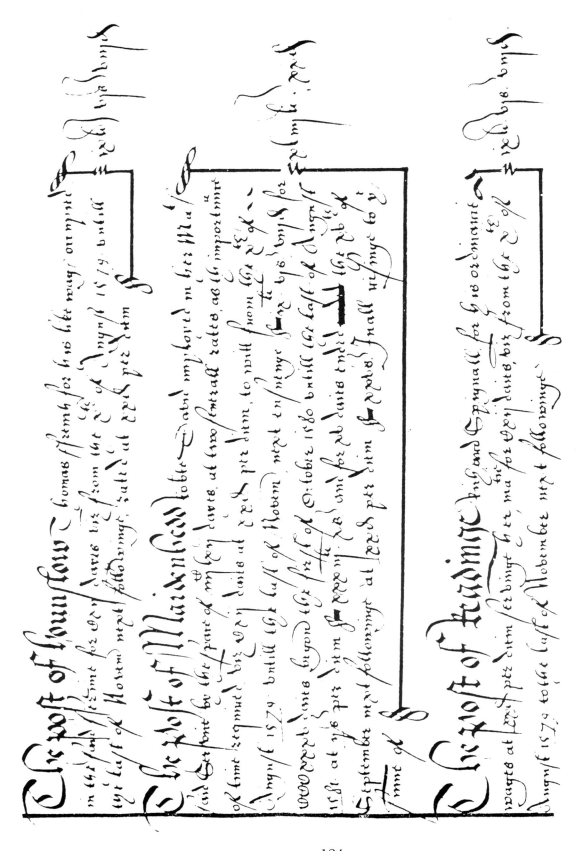

The Post was started by Henry VIII. But Elizabeth I began the service out of town and this is her order of 1579 for the mail 'towards Ireland from London to Bristol'. (Reproduced by permission of the Controller of HM Stationery Office).

To Shape a Town

Like all old English towns, Maidenhead was built from within. The Coopers, Woodbridges and Silvers did most of the physical building with local materials. Its laws began when a few leading townsmen made a few simple rules to control its market place with fair trading, and the first corporate properties were in land to produce income to meet the costs of bridge repairs. Magistrates and squires meted out a rough justice, and its first law officers included tithingmen to secure good behaviour on the streets. The churches began education and there was simple welfare for the poor through charities.

Churchmen, councillors, influential tradesmen, and wealthy landowners began to shape it into a town. Many of its institutions were to grow from benevolent efforts to help the poor and are rooted in the first borough charities for clothes, fuel, education, and housing. From there it developed its public undertakings—water, lighting and heating. Food came from local farms. Even when expanded into a flourishing town, it remained largely self-reliant and self-sufficient. Miraculously it escaped interference from outside forces between the wars, and Maidenhead and its mythology rolled on into the post-war years—until the Welfare State took it by surprise. Its institutions were created by voluntary initiative, then seized by the state in what seemed to old Maidonians a massive act of larceny. It even lost control of its own landscape to the Town & Country Planning Act. Newcomers eventually poured over the Bridge, the population doubling in a generation. The developers moved in and Victorian Maidenhead was bulldozed away. There were fears that the decade of demolishing and building and road making would wipe out everything of which the town was fond, and that the new people would destroy the old legends. Then a remarkable thing happened. Out of the gloom of uniformity came a piece of old extrovert Maidenhead in a new dress— the modern Central Library. It was designed by Paul Korelak.

Changes in the character of the streets began in 1836 when the lighting and watching committee requested the Gas Company to lay pipes to the Sun Inn, Moor Arches, North Town Road to High Street, and Back Lane (West Street). The Watching Committee dealt with law and order, but by 1855, the squires and magistrates were unable to cope with crime. The Crimean War had ended in September. There was a trade depression and universal distress. One person in every eleven was a pauper. Rioting and sedition were rife. In 1849, Colonel Vansittart of Cookham was to be the prime mover in the formation of a county constabulary. It was said that few went to bed without providing themselves with loaded firearms. Some 'put explosive balls round their premises'. Mr Sawyer of Bray, a county magistrate called a meeting in Maidenhead to discuss the formation of a police force. It was attended by landlords and farmers. Such was the feeling of insecurity for both life and property, that £180 was immediately subscribed for the establishment of a police force. It was Colonel Vansittart who persuaded Quarter Sessions in 1855 to set up the county constabulary.

In addition to widespread poverty, Maidenhead was on one of the great highways for tramps crossing the country and hundreds of arrests were made. As early as 1709, court records show many orders for the conveyance of vagrants. 'Elizabeth Kay and others, passed from London to Bristol, conveyed from Colnbrook to Maidenhead'. The descendants of the tithingmen became the special constabulary. On November 21, 1803, some 140 leading inhabitants of Maidenhead were sworn in as specials to meet the threat of a French invasion. But it was not until January 27, 1836, that the watch committee appointed four constables. Their original duties were to apprehend beggars for each of whom they received 2s 6d. In 1880, when two prisoners escaped from the Park Street lock-up, a public meeting was called to discuss this culpable negligence, and the whole force, except one man who was not on duty, was discharged. The Maidenhead Advertiser reported: 'The Borough Police system which has been upheld by half a century of jovial tradition and no end of patching and repair, thus came to an end in a day'. A new force under Inspector James Taylor of the Metropolitan Police was a great improvement.

Private enterprise started the Gas Company in 1835 and the Waterworks Company in 1875. Mayors and other local dignitaries sat on their boards of management. The electricity undertaking was set up by the council in 1897. Maidenhead was especially rich in water supplies, a good example being the artesian well at Nicholson's Brewery which was 400ft. deep. It has been sealed off and is under the new Shopping Precinct. The Brewery worked an emergency supply system for the hospital. Reeled flexible steel hose was rolled out across High Street, down the passage to the Portland Arms through which it passed on its way to Kidwells Park and the Hospital.

Neither gas nor electricity were fully understood by all when first introduced. A Mrs Atkinson of Holly Lodge Ray Park, followed by a domestic, went to investigate a smell of gas in her drawing-room, and, according to the Advertiser, proceeded to make tests with a lighted taper. 'Ultimately she stood upon a chair and applied the taper to the top of the chandelier'. Mrs Atkinson was blown off the chair and the domestic was hurled through the doorway into the passage, but escaped injury. The force of the explosion smashed the door to smithereens. Domestic servants were a hardy breed.

An Advertiser report concerning the beginning of electricity was published in 1902: 'Several residents and shop-keepers had their switches open to receive the light, and the suddenness of its appearance must have startled them as the hour at which the light was to be supplied was not known'. It was on December 9, 1902 that the Mayor (Major J. E. Pearce) switched on the first power station in Braywick Road. The report continued:

'There were 28 services ready for the new illuminant, which probably represented nearly 500 lights. Mrs Brown-Potter of Bray Lodge, Fishery Estate, had her switches open and was probably one of the first to get the light. We understand that this lady had nearly 200 lamps on her premises'. At first, electricity was only available between 2 pm and 6 am.

Electricity and gas were novelties, and so was standard time. Until the arrival of the railways with railway time, the nearest thing Maidenhead had to a time signal was Miss Belleville of 43 St Luke's Road, who distributed the correct time for a fee. Her chronometer was corrected at the Royal Observatory and her customers included business houses in the City, and clock and watch makers. The service was started by her father, who when he died in 1856, was making £500 a year at it. Watchmakers always wound the clocks in big houses and no doubt passed on Miss Belleville's correctness.

Education began with Merry's and Spoor's charities supporting a schoolmaster for the borough at £9 a year. They helped support the National Schools, founded in 1817, for the education of the poor in the principles of the established church. Schools were concerned with morality. Girls did knitting and the making-up and mending of clothes. The mistress got half the profit from the work as part-wages. There was a buyer's market in domestic servants. Until recent years, education was geared to commercial requirements; mid-nineteenth century schools were nurseries for clerks. The pupils could add and spell more accurately than any succeeding generation.

In 1848 the British School was started by Maidenhead Congregationalists. In 1863 the Wesleyan school appeared, adjoining the High Street Church. All Saints Schools opened in 1857, and the Catholic Schools in 1871. The British and Wesleyan Schools were superceded by Gordon Road School with the passing of the Balfour Act in 1902. The first boys' secondary school was built by the Maidenhead Commercial School Company in 1894 (the building became the Masonic Hall); the school became Desborough. The County Girls School, now Newlands, appeared in 1905.

Until the arrival of the Welfare State, government aid to schools was to supplement the activities of the family and the church, and to replace them only when they failed. Some state grants were paid on results, leading to a public examination of scholars in the Town Hall so that taxpayers could judge how their money was being spent. But they still had to pay to watch the embarrassment of the young scholars. A school attendance officer in 1905 said, 'every child missing a day at schools throws something like twopence on the rates'. During Ascot Week £16 in grants was lost through absence. There was passive resistance to changes in education when the state extended its influence. Church people, particularly non-conformists, refused to pay the education rate. Legal proceedings followed. Their goods were confiscated.

Real local control over education has now disappeared from state schools. The old buildings have been replaced, but in several of these, unlike the solid buildings of Victorian days, the roofs including that of the new Furze Platt school, were suspected as unsafe, and they were closed while remedial work was done.

One of the most solid of all basic Maidenhead institutions, reflecting the compassion of the town for its own people, was the Cottage Hospital. There was a love affair between the hospital and the town from the start. Victorian England was a place of unwholesome trades, excessive exertions by labourers, and often want of proper food and clothing, all of which led to disorders and inability to work. The sick poor were the problem of the age. When the breadwinner was unemployed the family starved. He was unable to meet the expense of lying-in.

Agitation for a hospital began in the 1870s, and was brought to a head by an accident on the railway line, where a man was found dying. There was a choice for those who found him, between jolting him 12 miles to Reading, or carrying him one-and-a-half miles to the Workhouse. The lesser evil was accepted. With his head hanging over a hurdle he was borne to the Workhouse. He died the next morning.

In 1877 half a dozen people met in Brock Lane Schoolroom, to launch a Cottage Hospital Fund. Maidenhead's population was 7,000. They made collecting boxes and went out to raise the money. On April 15, 1879 when they had collected £239-1s-4d, a procession formed outside the Town Hall with bands in attendance. They marched to Norfolk Park, the banners and regalia of the friendly societies giving the march some colour, the brass helmets of the fire brigade and the begowned Corporation adding a touch of authority to the occasion. John Hibbert of Braywick Lodge laid the foundation stone. There was a flood of gifts to equip it which included : sheets, brushes, an air cushion, clock and free winding of same, two bedsteads on Tingley's patent principle, £5 in ironmongery, 5 tons of coal, a bath, photographs for the walls, electric bell and fittings, a locker, 20 rhododendrons, and 14 volumes of The Illustrated London News. The hospital was built by Mr W. Woodbridge and by opening day had cost £1,350. There were rules. Only one patient could be recommended for every guinea subscribed, and no person was admitted without security from some substantial person for payment for burial or removal in cases of sudden emergency. Matron earned just under £1 a week; a nurse and servant shared £39-10s-10d a year. The hospital grew to have both maternity and children's wards and an impressive medical staff who gave their services free. But it was in constant financial trouble and eventually set up a contributory scheme not so different in aims to the National Health Scheme, yet to come with the Welfare State.

From the period that included the first world war and the years of depression which followed, local government concentrated on saving the rates rather than expanding services. There was no popular pressure upon the council because people believed progress came through voluntary initiative. In 1908 the Chamber of Trade advertised in the London newspapers that the rates had gone down by sixpence in the £ to 3s 6d. The Borough electricity undertakings was said to be saving the town a 4d rate, largely due as, it turned out, to economising on maintenance. When the SEB took it over it was said that some sections were about to blow up. In 1883, Alderman Loveridge proposed that when an assistant to the Town Clerk was appointed, the Town Clerk's salary should be reduced 'to furnish a proportion of the same'; and when Cookham RDC appointed a temporary surveyor in 1915, who was an 'early riser and total abstainer', he gave this undertaking : 'I will not try to introduce any new ideas'. The Public Libraries Act and main drainage were both resisted by the council, Councillor Frank Porter saying in 1906, that the council was wasting its money on main drainage. He was elected mayor three years later. They did eventually build the sewerage works, a stone's throw from the town.

Modern Maidenhead began after the second world war. So fast and so complete were the changes that old Maidenhead was practically destroyed. In the first years of peace there was a severe housing shortage, overcrowding, tuberculosis was beginning to take a hold in poor properties, the sewerage works was seriously polluting the Thames, and the volume of motor traffic was to bring the central triangle of High, Queen, and King Streets, into a stationary heap of hardware several times a day. Bill Nash, the King Street Florist installed a large electric fan in his shop near the traffic lights, to blow the petrol fumes away : they were killing the blooms. A new team of professional local government officers set about curing these problems. One of the signal successes of this period was the virtual ridding of the town of TB by the health department headed by Dr Brodie Moore. The campaign embraced everything from street cleaning and shop hygiene to slum clearance. A ring of council housing estates was built round the borders of the town. More than 2,000 families were rehoused. This was followed by model homes for the elderly. At the same time, small industrial estates for light industry were provided to secure local employment. The Maidenhead by-pass, begun in 1939 and abandoned at the outbreak of war, was built, and is now part of the M4. The Central Area Development Plan to a scheme by Lord Esher followed the building of the new Town Hall, opened by the Queen in 1962 and designed by Guy North of North & Partners, Maidenhead.

For some 20 years after the war the town was in an uproar of development. The people stood by in a daze and watched, and grumbled. In fact they were watching the rebirth of an old Thames-side town—something that had not happened here since the 19th century. These were pioneers of a different kind. The Victorians would have cheered this show of prosperity, but modern Maidenhead, weary of it all, just muttered and refused to take part. Not until this year has the town begun to take stock and join in, through the Maidenhead Look Ahead Committee.

One man more than any other is entitled to recognition as the architect of modern Maidenhead; Stanley Platt, formerly town clerk. He visualised a town cleanly and attractively housed, with first class social, cultural and commercial facilities. An astute administrator and a champion of Maidenhead, he is continuing public work in retirement. The road pattern upon which the new town is rising was planned by Charles Read, former Borough Surveyor, who still lives here in retirement. And up to re-organisation, Charles King managed the town's financial affairs with considerable advantage to its economy. The old borough came to an end on April 1, 1974 to become part of the Royal Borough of Windsor and Maidenhead.

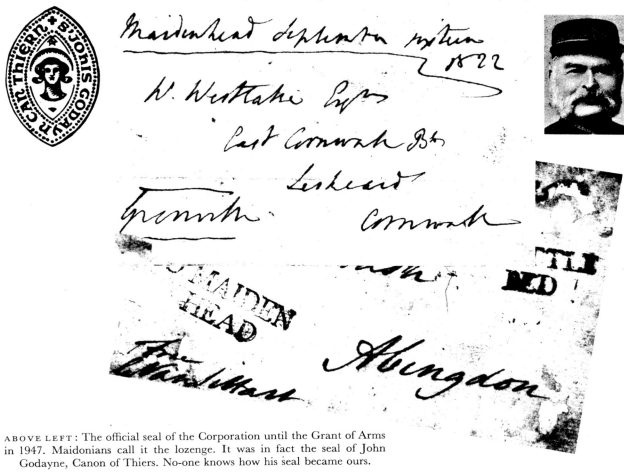

ABOVE LEFT: The official seal of the Corporation until the Grant of Arms in 1947. Maidonians call it the lozenge. It was in fact the seal of John Godayne, Canon of Thiers. No-one knows how his seal became ours.

ABOVE RIGHT: Head Constable Taylor.

CENTRE AND BELOW: Early letters were sent free if signed by someone who mattered; one carries the Earl of Orkney's signature. Another of 1785 that of George Vansittart, MP. (John Brooks).

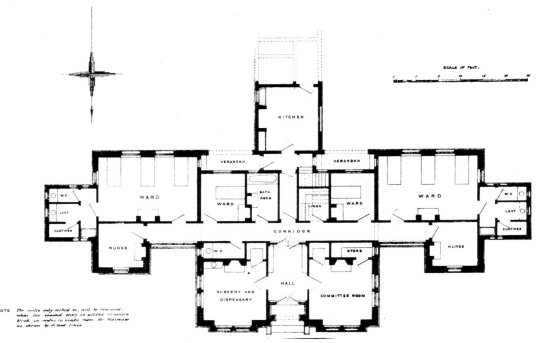

No.	Occupation.	Age.	Date of Admission.	Disease.	Date of Discharge.	Duration of illness.	Result.
				Cases treated since the opening of the Hospital—Nov. 6th, 1879.			
1	Paper Sorter	14	Nov. 22	Scalded Leg	Feb. 7	11 weeks	Cured
2	Hurdle-Maker... ...	40	Dec. 3	Broken Leg	Jan. 14	6 weeks	Cured
3	Child of Charwoman ...	5	,, 3	Sprained Ankle ...	Dec. 8	5 days	Relieved
3	Domestic Servant ...	31	,, 9	Tumour... ...	Dec. 29	3 weeks	Cured
5	Carpenter	30	,, 11	Broken Leg	Jan. 11	4½ weeks	Cured
6	Schoolmistress... ...	31	,, 27	Cystitis	,, 23	4 weeks	Cured
7	Domestic Servant ...	28	Jan. 4	Diseased Finger Bone	,, 13	1 week	Amputation, cured
8	Painter	33	,, 11	Enteris	,, 21	10 days	Cured
9	Painter	40	,, 19	Fistula	,, 27	8 days	Cured
10	Hurdle-Maker... ...	40	,, 24	Frozen Heel	Feb. 24	4½ weeks	Cured
11	Footman	19	,, 27	Tumour...	,, 24	4 weeks	Cured
12	Domestic Servant ...	35	Feb. 10	Pneumonia	March 2	3 weeks	Cured
13	Gardener	38	,, 16	Pneumonia			
14	Wife of Painter ...	30	,, 17	Fistula	,, 2	2 weeks	Successful Operation
15	Wife of Labourer ...	27	,, 17	Acute Rheumatism ...			
16	Errand-boy	18	,, 23	Ulcerated Leg			

ABOVE : Cottage Hospital elevation and plan.

BELOW : Cases treated.

ABOVE : John Budgen advertised in the 1880 brochure for the hospital's first year.

BELOW : So did W. J. Fry's Livery stables.

WALKER & SON,

PHARMACEUTICAL CHEMISTS,

ABOVE LEFT: Naturally Walker's the chemists offered their services when the hospital opened.

BELOW LEFT: Stuchbery & Thompson were last but not least in the hospital's booklet.

RIGHT: The small mace in silver gilt, dating from 1604— part of the Borough plate.

132

ABOVE: The old Guildhall.

BELOW LEFT: Beating the bounds.

BELOW RIGHT: D. Wilton, Captain of the Fire Brigade.

133

LEFT : The large mace, dated 1776.

ABOVE RIGHT : Maj J. E. Pearce introduced power to Maidenhead.

CENTRE : C. O. Milton was Borough electrical engineer.

BELOW RIGHT : Maidenhead Police station, Broadway.

ABOVE: Painters pose at the Grammar School.

BELOW: Gordon road School relay team, 1911.

THE MAIDENHEAD
DAILY BULLETIN.

Containing Official Local and Broadcast News.

No. 5   WEDNESDAY, MAY 12th, 1926.   ONE PENNY

Editorial.

The ninth day of the strike leaves our little town in a peaceful condition.

There is little or no disorganisation of life, indeed, the only hardship appears to be the shortage of coal, and this falls mostly on the poorest of the population.

The volume of food transport through the town has been enormous and has been admirably managed by the police. What a blessing the suggested relief road would have been at this juncture!

Until the London newspapers are able to supply adequately the general desire for news of the day's doings we shall continue to issue our little sheet each evening, which seems to be much appreciated in the town and neighbouring villages.

To-day's City Prices.

Paris Exchange 155, New York 4·86⅛, 5 p.c. War Loan 100, Gt. Western 86¼.

Weather Forecast.

Moderate to fresh S.W. winds. Occasional showers; bright periods. Visibility moderate to good. Moderate temperature. Further outlook unsettled.

Union Benefits.

CANNOT BE WITHHELD FROM WORKERS.

"It is a very common thing to find in the rules of a trade union . . . a rule to say that if a trade unionist does not obey the orders of the Executive of his Union he forfeits his benefits.

It cannot be too widely and plainly known that there is no court in this country which would ever construe such a rule as meaning that the man would forfeit his benefits if he is asked to do that which is wrong and illegal."—*Sir John Simon, in the House of Commons.*

To-day's News.

While there are many individual cases of strikers in various trades and services returning to work, the general strike continues unabated throughout the country. The success of the authorities in maintaining the feeding and vital services of the people must not obscure this grave fact, or its increasingly wasteful consequences to all classes.

The War Office announces that officers at home on leave from abroad may accept any form of employment in the present emergency that will not interfere with their military obligations or returning to their units at the end of their leave.

A message from King's Bay, Spitsbergen, states that the airship "Norge" started for the North Pole at 10.10 yesterday morning.

"ALL FED UP."—Two "specials" were engaged in patrol duty round a factory on the south side of the Thames, where strong strike pickets had been ordered by the union. Gradually they faded away, telling the "specials" that they were "fed up." In a short time there was none left but the man in charge of the pickets, and he requested the "specials" to inform any of his men who might appear that they could go home, adding, "We are all fed up."

In the House of Commons yesterday the Ministry of Pensions Vote was discussed in Committee, and later Sir John Simon again raised the question of the legality of the strike and made certain suggestions for a settlement. In the House of Lords the Economy Bill was dealt with in Committee.

The tendency of strikers to dribble back to work was accentuated yesterday, particularly among railway men and workers in the printing trades.

Shipyard and engineering workers on the Clyde, the Tyne, on Merseyside and at Cardiff have been called out, though the T.U.C. General Council disclaim responsibility for this action.

Freight trains are being more freely run and the distribution of food supplies to the London markets and throughout the country is proceeding satisfactorily.

The Government seized yesterday under its emergency powers a quantity of the stock of paper available for printing *The Times*.

An Emergency Regulation has been made with the object of preventing imported funds from being used in this country for any purpose prejudicial to the public safety.

Injunctions were granted by Mr. Justice Astbury, in the Chancery Division yesterday, to restrain until trial or further order, the officials of two branches of the National Seamen's and Firemen's Union from calling out their members on strike without a ballot under the rules. The Judge ruled that the so-called general strike was illegal.

As regards the strike position generally, the number of individuals returning to work is increasing, and in some cases considerable bodies of strikers have applied for re-instatement. On the other hand, there is, as yet, little sign of a general collapse of the strike, and the Trades Union Council is believed to be making efforts to call out certain trades still at work. It can be, however, definitely stated that there is a growing dissatisfaction among the strikers with the policy of a general strike, and considerable uneasiness as to its ultimate results.

The Corn factors at Mark Lane yesterday, decided not to raise prices of flour.

There are large supplies of fish in Manchester at lower prices than before the strike.

A Committee has been appointed to fix the maximum prices of eggs. Such prices as have been arranged should enable retailers to sell eggs at the same prices as those ruling before the strike.

During the first week of the British strike 600 Rhine barges, with a cargo of approximately one million tons of Ruhr coal, have arrived at Rotterdam. Great quantities of coal are being loaded for Scandinavian, Baltic and Mediterranean ports to meet the demands which are usually supplied by the British mining industry.

Stock Exchange business is quiet, but there is no alarm and the tone remains firm. Acting on the advice given, there has not been much selling of securities and an increasing cheerfulness is reported.

No pickets are at the gates of Woolwich Arsenal and several thousands of workers have returned without disturbance.

PEACE MOVEMENT.—The special meeting of the General Council of the T.U.C. and the Miners' Executive adjourned at 1.30 a.m. this morning. Mr. Cook told a press representative that there was no change in the situation, but the session was to continue at 10 a.m. this morning. Previous to the meeting of General Council, the Miners' Executive had met the Labour Leaders, and Mr. Ramsay Macdonald and Mr. Bevan accompanied them to the meeting. Mr. Cook stated yesterday—"Numbers of people have been approaching the Miners' Officials with a view to getting a settlement of the deadlock. I desire to repeat again what I said at New Cross on Sunday—peace is possible at any moment on terms which will give economic security to the miners."

The ample protection afforded by the Government to food transport, the police court actions, and the restraining efforts of the Trades Union Leaders, have combined to keep the country quiet.

TO assist in meeting the production costs of this sheet, the charge for this space is defrayed by Mr. A. S. Lidiard, Consulting Optician, 3, King Street, Maidenhead.

General Strike newspaper—1926.

ABOVE: Maidenhead Library—before.

BELOW: The new library.

137

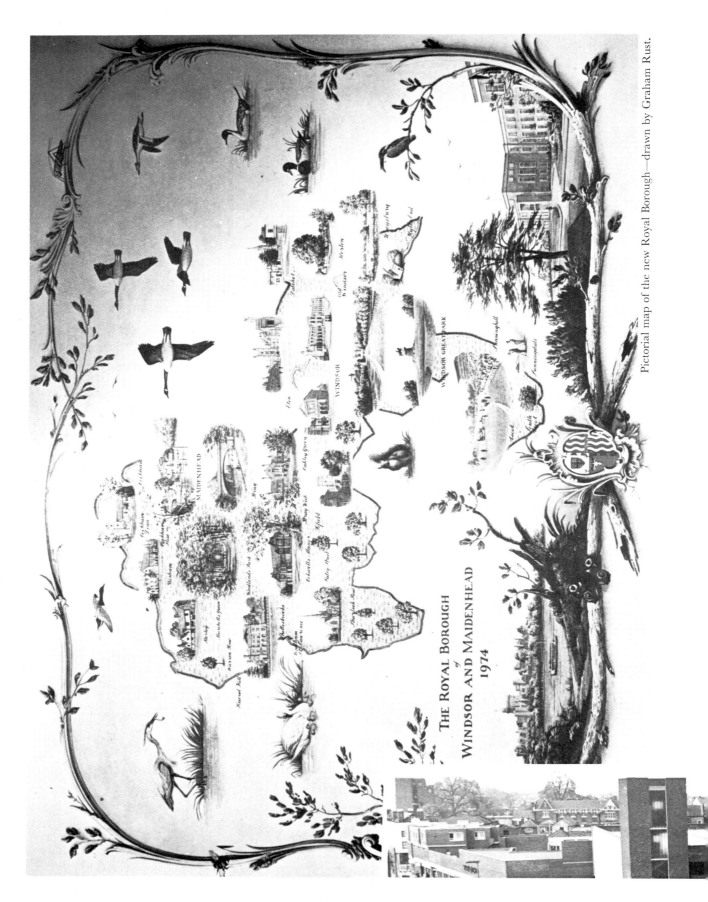

Pictorial map of the new Royal Borough—drawn by Graham Rust.

Current Affairs

Come the 1970s, Maidenhead was suffering from over-exposure to redevelopment and the supermarket way of life. There was a desperate need for a Canon Drummond to dress the people down. Hooliganism was rife, and aerosol paint sprays were leaving their marks on private gateways and public buildings. An incredible number of telephone kiosks, illuminated road direction signs, and other fragile street furniture, car parking machinery, public lifts, subway walls, and public places suffered disfigurement. Even psychiatrists were baffled by the rise in juvenile crime. The Crime Prevention Panel turned its attention to restraining shop-lifting. Readily portable electronic goods were secured by chains to display shelves. But a new Maidenhead began to emerge through the dust of demolition. Having largely re-housed the town, the council began to embellish it with attractive parks. A civic society was started for the purpose of involving townspeople in the changes and to make social improvements when the builders left. The parks department was set up under Edward L. Bond to landscape the new Maidenhead, which included developing the riverside gardens. The Central Area Scheme, which has suffered some amendments, has provided a traffic free High Street which has been attractively planted. Eventually, most of the central area will be free of traffic and paved from King Street to St Mary's Church. The relief roads, built to make this possible, will eventually be carried on to meet today's Braywick Road through a new arch in the railway embankment. In the Strategy for the South (the government paper on the future of planning), Maidenhead is in a recreational area. Accommodation for tourism therefore becomes a part of planning, especially in trying to preserve our attractive villages. It is also thought that the shorter working week will bring a demand for more leisure pursuits.

Distinctive changes in the skyline have been brought about by the town's first tower block on the site of the old Town Hall, the new offices of the South of England Building Society, which incorporates the old Maidenhead Permanent Benefit Building Society, and new office blocks in the town centre. The new Town Hall has become the administrative headquarters of the new Royal Borough of Windsor and Maidenhead, with HRH The Prince

Maidenhead's new skyline, 1975.

139

of Wales as High Steward. Thus the little settlement on the edge of Windsor Forest, whose affairs had been dominated and shaped by royal office holders of Windsor Castle in its earliest days, had found itself in a similar sort of unity, with the seat of power remarkably transferred to Maidenhead. The dominant physical features have remained the same: the river and the main road to the west.

A light planning touch can be found in the Lower Cookham Road scheme, that would have done credit to our early builders. The parks department created Ray Mill Island, and have done their best to green-belt the town. The relief roads brought into focus a waste area from Forlease Road to Marlow Road, which is being developed in the modern idiom. The largest building there is the Leisure Centre. It is an extension of the Old Drill Hall, later called Pearce Hall after J. D. M. Pearce, who set up the Kidwells Park Trust. The Pearce Hall site was sold to the Commonwealth War Graves Commission, who built their prestige headquarters there. The money from the sale has gone into the Centre, which is being linked to a new multi-storey car park by an over-head footway. The car park stands on William Hamblett's swimming pool site. The new police station and fire and ambulance headquarters are being completed near Forlease roundabout by J. M. Jones & Sons. The firm was founded by John Markham Jones who came to Maidenhead at the turn of the century. It is now a group of eleven companies operating throughout the South East. The town's Western Approaches over the Thicket are protected by the Maidenhead and Cookham Commons Committee of the National Trust. Where the highwaymen used to ride there are gallops and green glades. From the east the approach is along a relandscaped Braywick Road. The shrubs were especially chosen to make this a golden way. There are views across Braywick Sports Grounds and the beautiful open-planned Braywick Park, once John Hibbert's home. The light industrial estates, and a planned factory development, make up the town's industry. Clustered near the M4 but in country settings are such famous names as Hacker Radio, a Maidenhead firm founded by the brothers Hacker, making high quality electronic equipment, Vandervell, Brylcreem, and the European headquarters of the American publishing concern McGraw Hill.

The riverside, traditional home of fun and games, has adapted to modern times and there is heavy pleasure boat traffic. A new restaurant, Boulters Inn, which opened since the war, is now Corporation property, being part of Ray Mill Island, and there is a new inland hotel—Esso—at Shoppenhangers Manor, which is drawing some of the banqueting trade away from the river. Inn-keeping has changed too. There is a sprinkling of international custom from the closeness of London Airport, with US greenbacks turning up in hotel tills.

If anything, the artistic population has expanded through music and drama festivals, the highspot being the Cookham Village Festival which brings international talent to this Thames-side site. Modern Maidenhead is more outward looking than the old, with strong European links through the twin towns of Saint-Cloud, Bad Godesberg, and Frascati. In recognition of this, it won the European Flag in 1965. In some ways this is an extension of Viscount Astor's intentions at Cliveden, when he set out to make that a place where different nationals could meet.

Maidenhead will continue to cater for the new leisured classes of the shorter working week. Planning is directed towards conserving the natural beauty of the villages. The Mayor of the Royal Borough, Councillor Kit Aston, whose council has the responsibility of carrying on, used the term 'cherish' when he made it clear that the council's concern is to continue to improve amenities for the people who live in and around Maidenhead.

ABOVE: The key to the Town Hall—opened by
HM Queen Elizabeth in June 1962.

ABOVE: The last Borough Council. Back Row—Alan Gillott, D. S. Thomas (housing manager), John Brown, Dr R. M. Lazlett (medical officer), Roy Close, Dennis Jones (chief public health officer), Eric Brooks, Fred Garrett (mace bearer), Cedric Harrop, Harry Mills (borough surveyor), Derek Bignold, Edward L. Bond (parks superintendent), John D. Barton, Charles King (borough treasurer), Fred Allgood, Neville Whiteley. Sitting—Harry Griffin, John Neve, Harold Neve (alderman emeritus), Stanley Croxford (deputy mayor), Mrs Euphemia Underhill (mayor), Stanley Platt (town clerk), the Rev Michael McGowan (mayor's chaplain), Tom Bailey, Joyce Fotherby.

BELOW LEFT: Former High Steward John Smith and his wife.

BELOW RIGHT: Councillor Mrs Euphemia Underhill, last Mayor of the Borough of Maidenhead. (John Neal).

141

Royal visitors to a Royal Borough: LEFT: The Queen comes ashore at Cookham, during her historic journey in October 1974. RIGHT: HRH the Prince of Wales is installed High Steward of the new Royal Borough. BELOW: High Steward's Barge, formerly that of Jesus College, Oxford.

ABOVE: Maidenhead Town Hall, administrative headquarters of the
Royal Borough of Windsor and Maidenhead.

CENTRE: Paving has replaced the old Bath road through High street.

BELOW: New Leisure Centre and indoor swimming pool.

143

A Change of Programme

Change in terms of urban landscape since the war, which all but obliterated Victorian Maidenhead, was always resented but in a sense understood. The 1980s brought a much more significant and complicated change, something which has nothing to do with the view and everything to do with the future in both commercial and domestic situations. Maidenhead is no longer a small town minding its own business but a growing commercial centre with international links.

Just as the landscaping of so much urban change by former Parks Superintendent Edward Bond was taking on an air of maturity, softening the memory of the upheavals, Maidenhead was called upon to adjust to computerisation. The original concept of light industrial estates on the outskirts was shattered. The electronics industry moved into the town centre from America and elsewhere. Bits, bytes, and binary numbers suddenly became part of school conversation. Old Maidenhead, including the Chamber of Commerce, whose roots were with the old mayors and aldermen of High Street trading, was non-plussed. The Chamber even opposed a planning application for a software shop. But there was no resisting the new force. Worst of all, Maidenhead, as it turned out, seemed to be leading the way into a new era of communications. Taplow Court, on the Great Hill of Mai Dun, where an earlier beginning had been made, was to reassert its historical importance. In rooms where kings and queens were entertained by the Desboroughs, Plessey technologists, led by Bill Tulloch, produced System X, a digital telephone system which was thought to be the world's best, and they pioneered the use of optical fibre cables (no thicker than a human hair) along which telephonic communication passed in light signals.

The first of these cables ran from Maidenhead to Slough. Over it travels speech, facsimile, graphics and computer data. It revolutionised communication by telephone, the network upon which the computer industry is based. British Telecom are currently installing this system nationwide.

Years before, J.D.M. Pearce, founder of Craufurd College, had tried to interest Maidenhead youth in electricity and magnetism. His college produced some of the pioneers of the industry, which gives the town an historical link with today's world of electronics.

So Maidenhead, still reeling from the architectural change from local bricks to imported concrete, could only stand on the bank and watch as a new generation of people and ideas flooded into familiar places, overspilling into shops and schools. Lured by the London Airport M-way link, the flood tide brought international business. UK and European headquarters of famous corporations rose in unlikely places. Most significantly, Maidenhead has become part of the largest data processing community in Europe. This change in the town's business life was to have a greater influence upon its future than anything the Victorians had done. One feels that the Victorians would have thoroughly approved of such enterprise.

It happened, as things often do with computers, at considerable speed. King Street, last bastion of private trading, was rebuilt. Zilog from Silicon Chip Valley, California, moved in, later to build their UK headquarters in Moorbridge Road. A British company, Travicom set up shop there. The world's airlines were queuing for their booking systems. A Maidenhead couple set up Decision Support Systems over Stanley Peake's shop and within a year were exporting. Down the road the US giant Management Science America built new offices. Just round the corner Philips Business Systems did the same. Headmaster Graham Sullivan of Lowbrook Primary School, Cox Green, introduced his pupils, including 5-year-olds, to computers. It started when a woman won a Commodore Pet in a competition. Lowbrook was soon copywriting its own educational programmes for export to other schools and attracted the attention of the international press.

This led to Micro Scope Ltd lending the school a programmer. Set up by Chris Sealy and Paul Shimmel in Mill Lane, Taplow, this company was to lead the world in videotex systems in Europe, Australasia, and North America.

In Berkshire House — the old town hall site — George Hudson founded Topas. They automated the Esso terminal in Greece and came to dominate the world market in their field — the bulk distribution of liquids. Both companies were founded by the generation of young men who produced application software here, which was to power the new information technology.

When J. M. Jones, the construction group, moved out of Reliance House, Leasco Software Ltd moved in. When the Royal Navy went to war in the Falklands the ships were equipped with their BRITMISS system, enabling shore HQ to provide commanders at sea with the position of distant vessels. This was another first.

The 1980s also saw the spread of computers as tools to High Street retail shops; in some cases these computers, through connection to the telephone system provided two-way communication with host computers at wholesale depots. Leasco devised a similar system for pharmacists, now in use nationwide, and Micro Scope a machine that translates pharmacists' Latin shorthand into English and prints medicine bottle labels. Both devices do lots of other things as well. The *Advertiser* computerised its printing works, and the Town Hall set up a technology group of officers to explore ways of improving local administration.

In 1987, Berkshire County Library Service installed a viewdata terminal in Maidenhead Library. It was one of the first of many to provide a public information service which is also being carried by Windsor Television, who are currently cabling up Maidenhead.

But one of the most powerful influences upon the new technology in the higher echelons of electronics came from St Mark's Road, where John Ceresa, long-time resident of the town, manages a company which makes instruments essential to technological advance — Racal Dana. The story of Maidenhead's move into data processing would be incomplete without a reference to Max Lipman's Moorbridge Road company LMR, among the first to encourage businessmen to explore the advantages of computers as business tools.

But of all local industry's achievements in recent years, one project stands out — the building of the Thames Barrier, which has been described as a new engineering wonder of the world. The design work for this was done in Costain's offices above the Precinct by a team led by John Reeve. Industrial prosperity led to pressure for more accommodation for local companies, whose variety of work stretched from making parts for North Sea oil rigs and Concorde, to Mike Hope's Concept Engineering on the old Saxon estate at White Waltham Airfield. There they make special effects for the film industry, including the Bond epics.

A general liveliness in the Maidenhead industrial scene led to pressure upon the council to provide more accommodation for small industrial and commercial companies, and in 1987 they opened a new estate off Stafferton Way. This in a period of prolonged recession, reflected the buoyancy of business here. Once again, local geography is probably at the root of it all — excellent communications. Looking back the town seems to have moved forward in 100 year cycles. Coaching spanned about that period. Private trading in the High Street is another example. It was in the 1880s that the Victorians brought a wave of prosperity to the town which changed its character. The 1980s may well be a comparable example. We are at the beginning of a new century for Maidenhead. It will be a century of immense social change, when the town sheds rather more of its parochialism than it has ever done before. But this should not change the heart of the place. Continuity lies with the old Maidenhead families.

Government by the re-organised local authority has unfortunately become extremely party-political, and in some sense more remote. Perhaps the County's viewdata system will become something of an antidote. Real adjustment to social and commercial change is being attempted in the schools, who have undoubtedly moved rather faster than the general public believes, towards meeting the demands that the future may bring. To aid this process a schools-industry partnership was set up. The first Chairman of the Maidenhead Committee was Eric Lacy, headmaster of Cox Green Comprehensive School. It has been extremely successful in changing attitudes, so much so that similar committees elsewhere have been formed on the same lines.

What is not extraordinary is that Maidenhead should have become a substantial contributor to what has been called the Second Industrial Revolution. The Thames, the Bath Road, Brunel's railway, the M4, have kept us in the main stream of events, which helped to shape the country's history — we even had an axe factory in prehistoric times. So why shouldn't we be part of the largest data processing community in Europe? It must be decreed by the geography of the place.

Bibliography

Lower Palaeolithic Archaeology in Britain by John Wymer
Ice Ages, their Nature and Effects by Ian Cornwall
Upper Thames Region by J. R. L. Anderson
Anglo Saxon Burials in the Middle Thames
Romano British Settlement in the Thames Valley ⎱ by Luke Over
Romano British Influence in the Maidenhead Area ⎰
The Thames Highway by F. S. Thacker
Hundred of Bray by Charles Kerry
A History of Maidenhead by Wesley Walker
Bray Today and Yesterday by Nan Birney
Tribal Feeling by Michael Astor
Nancy Astor by Maurice Collis
The Picture Book of Brasses in Gilt by Henry Trivick
One Hundred Years Berkshire Constabulary by W. Indge
Brief Glory, the story of ATA by E. C. Cheeseman

Index (*Third Edition*)

Advertiser 145	Decision Support	Management Science	Sealy, Chris 145
Bath Road 146	System 144	America 144	Shimmel, Paul 145
Berkshire House 145	High Street 146	Micro Scope Ltd. 145	Stafferton Way 145
Bond, Edward 144	Hope, Mike 145	Moorbridge Road 144, 145	Sullivan, Graham 144
British Telecom 144	Hudson, George 145	Pearce, J.D.M. 144	System X 144
BRITMISS System 145	Jones, J.M. 145	Philips Business	Taplow Court 144
Brunel 146	Lacy, Eric 146	Systems 145	Thames Barrier 145
Ceresa, John 145	Leasco Software Ltd. 145	Plessey 144	Topas 145
Concorde 145	Lipman, Max 145	Racal Dana 145	Town Hall (old) 145
Costain 145	Lowbrook Primary	Reliance House 145	Travicom 144
Cox Green 144	School 146	St Mark's Road 145	Tulloch, Bill 144
Cox Green Comprehensive	LMR 145	St Mary's House 145	Windsor Television 145
School 146	Mai Dun,	Schools Industry	Zilog 144
Desboroughs 144	Great Hill of 144	Partnership 146	

Index

A

Adams, Bob	112
Advertiser	90
Advertiser Trust	91
Aella	14
Air Raids	59
Air Transport Aux.	59
Alden, Bob	112
Aldrea of Dorney	21
Alfred, King	13
All Saints' Avenue	13
All Saints' Church	33
Altwood	39
Altwood Bailey kilns	14
Altwood Works	90
Alward the Goldsmith	22
Animals, prehistoric	13
Anderson, Gerry	113
Andrews family	65
Ann of Cleaves	22
Anti-parachute patrols	60
Ascot Sunday	67
Asgot of Taplow	21
Asquith, ex-PM	60
Aston, Councillor Kit	140
Astor family	79
Astor, Nancy	59, 67, 113
Astor, Viscount	59, 67
Austin Canons	22
Axes, stone age	13

B

Bacon factory	92
Bapsey Pond	15
Baptist Church	33
Barford & Norkett	112
Barge horses	64
Barges decline	64
Barry, Sir Edward	77
Battings	90, 94
Baylis, Fdk.	92
Baylis Louis	92
Bear Hotel	34, 40
Belgic fort	14
Belgium evacuees	59
Belmont Park Avenue	13
Benedictine Abbey	22, 40
Berkshire College of Agri.	30
Berkshire Downs	14
Berry, Manor of	22
Beynhurst Hundred	21
Bibroci	14
Biggs, E. T.	89, 91
Black Death	29
Blue Ribbon Army	42
Boathouse leases	65
Bodleian Library	77
Bodley, Sir Thos.	77
Boer War	60
Bomanji, Sir Dhunjibhoy	68
Bombs	59
Bond, Edward L.	139
Bond, Jonathan	65
Bondi, of Bisham	21
Borough Church	39
Boulter's Inn	140
Boulter's Lock	63
Boxall, Sir Charles	66
Boyne Hill	13
Bray	13
Bray Studios	113
Bray, Vicar of	39
Braywick	13, 14
Braywick Road	14
Braywick Sports Ground	140
Bridge	63
Bridge House	112
Bridge tolls, misappropriation	40
Bridgemasters	40
Brill, Edward	94

Brisson, Carl	111
Bristol & Exeter Mail	41
Britain, Festival of	68
Britannia PH	60
British restaurant	60
Brock Lane	92
Brown & Such	94
Brown, Daniel Hubert	94
Brown, John	94
Brown, Major	42
Bruton, Eric	77
Buckhounds, Royal	39
Budgen, John	92, 93
Builders	125
Building Society	139
Bulle Inn	22, 40
Burgin, Eric	77
Burnham, Jas.	89, 91
Burnham, Wm.	91
Bushnell, John	111
Bustleham, Manor of	22
Butler's Stores	92
By-pass	128

C

Calleva Atrabatus	14
Camlet Way	14
Canadian Red Cross Hospital	59
Candlemaking	92, 93
Canhurst Farm	14
Cannon Court Farm	13
Canon Hill	15
Canteen, services	60
Carpentier, George	112
Carter, Mr & Mrs George	9
Castle Hill villa	14
Celts	13
Chapel Arches	43
Chapel of ease	39
Charities	126
Charles I	29, 129
Charter, Elizabeth I	40
Chauntry chapel	40
Cherry, Francis	25
Cherry gardens	42
Christians, first	15
Churchill, Winston	67
Cinema	113
Clare Road	94
Clayton, Sir Robt.	30
Clayton-East, Sir G.	64
Cliveden	21, 66, 79
Cliveden Hospital	59, 79
Cliveden Set	67
Cliveden Stud	79
Coaching	35
Cock-fighting	42
Coffin, Richard	30
Colonnade	94
Compton, Earl of	29
Concrete houses	79
Congregational Church	33
Cooke, Rev. John	33
Cookham	13
Cookham Bridge	42
Cookham Festival	140
Cookham Rise	13
Cookham Road	59
Cordwallis Estate	113
Council, first	40
Counties, start of	15
Courage's Brewery	92
Court, Walter	93
Courthouse Road	13
Courtlands	13, 90

Courtnidge, Cecelie	68
Courts, furnishers	93
Cox Green	14
Craufurd Estate	79
Cresswells, Manor of	22
Cricket	42, 92, 101
Crispin Miles	22
Cromwell, Oliver	29
Cromwell Road	13
Cromwell's Army	29
Cruising	64
Cusack-Smith, Sir Berry	77
Cycle industry	94

D

Dahlias	94
Danby, Earl of	29
Danes	13, 15
David, Robt., postmaster	41
Desborough, Baron	23, 64, 67, 68
Desborough, estate	23, 79
Desborough, Lady	67
Devonshire, Earl of	29
Dimbleby, Richard	77
Domesday	21
Dorney Court	90
Double Nick	92
Dragoons, Irish	30
Drainage, street	41
Drummond, Canon	113
Dumb Bell Station	64
Dumb Bell, Taplow	13
Dunkirk, little ships	60
Dunn, Never Never	89
Dutch children	60
Dutch, PM	59

E

Ealdorman Aelfheah	21
Early settlers	21
East Street	91
Edinburgh, Duke of	60
Edith, Queen	21
Edward, the Confessor	15
Edward VII	65
Eel bucks	64
Eglington, Wm.	77
Eisenhower, General	112
Electricity	79, 126
Elizabeth I	23
Elizabeth, Princess (1647)	29
Elizabeth II, River progress	68
Ellington, Manor of	22
Ellwood, Thos.	30
Elmslie School	94
English Church	15
Esgar the Staller	21
Esher, Lord	128
Esso Hotel	140
Evacuees	59

F

Fairey Aviation	60
Fairs	40
Fane, Ethel Anne	78
Farmers, first	13
Feen's Farm	14
Ferriers, Henry de	22
Field system, first	13, 14
Fifield	59
Film studios	113
Fire Brigade	60
First people	13
Flash lock	63
Flint industry	13
Floods	68

Folijohn Park	59
Forest, Windsor	39
Fourleys	40
Foxleys	23
Fredrick, Prince of Wales	67
Freeman, Hardy & Willis	93
Furze Platt	13, 59

G

Gage, Viscount	78
Garke, Emile	78
Gas Co.	41, 125, 126
George Inn, Bray	67
German prisoners	59
Geys Manor	77
Giacomo	79
Glacier, Bourne End	13
Gloucester, Duke of (1647)	29
Gloucester Mail	41
Gold ornaments	14
Gooch, Daniel	64
Gordon Road School	77
Greasepaint Special	111
Great Western Rly	64, 42
Great West Road	39
Greenfields	94
Grenfell family	23, 78
Grenfell, Wm. Henry (see Desboro)	78, 93
Gresley, Rev Wm.	34
Greyhound Inn	29
Guardians, Board of	42
Guards Boat Club	66
Gude, Geo.	94
Guild, SS Andrew & Mary	40
G.W.K. cars	113

H

Hall Place	30
Hamblett, Wm.	91
Hamblettonian Hall	91, 95
Hand, David	113
Harold, King	22
Haven of Rest	112
Hearn, Thos.	77
Hermon, S. R.	93
Herring, Geo.	112
Heybournes	92, 113
Heywood Park	22
Hibbert, John	79, 128
Higgs, John	33, 34, 42
High Steward's Barge	112
High Street pioneers	90
Highwaymen	40
Hinds Head Hotel, Bray	112
Hippodrome	94
Hoby family	22
Home Guard	60
Horsham family	65
Hosebond family	39
Hosebond John	40
Hospital	59, 126, 127
Hughes, Miss Joan	59
Hundreds	21
Hungaria	66, 112
Hurley, Manor of	21
Hurley Priory	23

I

Ice wells	91
Ice House	91
Ickneild Way	14
Industry	128, 140
International Stores	93
Isaac's Stores	91
Islet Park	113
Ive, Manor of	22
Ive, John	22
Ives Place	22

J

James I	39, 41
Jesus Hospital	77
Jewish community	34

Johnson, Amy 59
Jones, John Markham .. 140
Jones, J. M. & Sons .. 140
Juliana, Princess.. .. 60

K
Kidwells Park .. 14, 101
Kidwells Park Trust .. 140
Kimbers 59
King George VI Club .. 94
Kitchener, Lord 79
Knight Ellington .. 21
Knights Templars .. 22
Korelak, Paul 125

L
Laburnham Road .. 94
Ladye Place 23
Lamb & Co. 90
Lampthorne, Richard .. 30
Langhorne, Nancy .. 79
Lassall, Wm. 78
Lehmann, John 77
Leicester, Earl of.. .. 29
Leisure Centre 140
Leland's Papers 77
Library, Central.. 22, 125
Library, first 91
Linden Avenue 13
Litkie, Arnold 77
Littlewick 39
London, City of 63
Lords, reform of 78
Lovegrove, R. 41
Lovelace, Lord .. 29, 30
Lumley, Earl of 29

M
McIlroys.. 92
Maidenhead, name .. 21
Maidenhead Bridge 30, 39, 40
Maidenhead FC 111
Manchester, Earl of .. 29
Mandeville, Geoffrey de 22
Manors 15, 21
Marandaz, Capt. .. 113
March, John 66
Market 40
Mary, Queen 89
Mattingley, Mr & Mrs G. 68
Mattingley, Nora .. 68
MCC 42
Mead, Carlton 77
Mead, Reggie 95
Messum, Geoffrey .. 60
Methodist Church .. 33
Mettyngham, Thos. .. 40
Midland Bank 40
Misener, Laurence .. 34
Mollison, Jim 59
Moor Farm .. 13, 113
Moore, Dr Brodie .. 128
Moores, James 89
Mooring rights 65
Morgan, H. F. S. .. 113
Morkar, Earl 21
Moss, Mr & Mrs A. E. .. 113
Moss, Stirling 113
Motor industry 113
Mounted Micks 30
Museum treasures .. 59
My Lady Ferry 64

N
Nash, Bill 128
National Trust .. 79, 140
National Westminster Bank 29
Neame, Barry 112
Neve, John 91
Neve, Julius .. 33, 91
New Road, Bourne End.. 13
Newry, Viscount .. 65
Nicholson, Robt. 90, 92

Nicholson, Wm. .. 90, 92
Nicholson's Brewery
42, 91, 92, 126
Nicholson's Lane .. 92
Night Clubs 112
Norkett's Dam 112
Normans 15
Norreys, Sir John .. 22
Norreys, Ricardo de .. 22
North Star 64
North Town 21

O
Ockwells.. 22
Odo, Bishop 22
Old Bell, Hurley .. 112
Olympic medal 111
Omnibus company .. 91
Oppenheimer family .. 77
Orange, Prince of 29, 30
Orkney Arms 66
Orkney, Earl of .. 23, 63
Outfall works 41
Oxford Crew 65
Oysters 14

P
Palmer, Sir Roger .. 65
Pearce Hall 140
Pearce, J. D. M. 42, 79, 140
Pearce, Maj J. E. .. 79
Penn Farm 33
Pepys, Samuel 30
Perma frost 13
Philibert, Hugo St .. 22
Picquigny 22
Pie Poudre, Court of .. 40
Pineapple Brewery .. 90
Pinkney, Ghilo de 15, 22
Pinkney, Manor of .. 22
Pitcher, Mrs Margaret .. 94
Platt, Stanley 129
Pocock family 77
Police 125, 126
Police force sacked .. 126
Police pay 78
Pollution.. .. 64, 128
Popperinge, Belgium .. 66
Porter, Frank 128
Portland Arms 126
Portledge Papers .. 30
Post, origin 41
Powney family 22
Precinct, Shopping 91, 92, 126
Protest groups 42
Public rights, erosion .. 63
Punch Magazine .. 77

Q
Quaker Rous 89
Queen Street Green .. 90

R
Racecourse .. 41, 42
Radclyffe, Edward Arnold 77
Railway fares 64
Raleigh, Sir Walter .. 29
Ray, Richard 63
Ray Lodge 77
Ray Mead Hotel 64, 112
Ray Mill 63
Ray Mill Island .. 68, 139
Read, Charles T. .. 129
Reginald de Maidenhuth 22
Relief committee .. 42
Revolt, 1688 29
Rheinbold the Priest .. 21
Ridgeway 14
Rioting 125
River ecology 64
Riviera Hotel 66
Robin Hood's Arbour .. 14
Robinson family .. 77

Rodger's foundry .. 90
Roller skating .. 91, 94
Roman bath 14
Roman roads 14
Roman villa 93
Romans 13
Rotodyne 60
Rowing Club 68
Royal Berkshire Nursery 94
Royalty, foreign .. 59
Rule Britannia 67
Rushworth Records .. 29
Russell, Earl of .. 29
Rustic Theatre, Cliveden 67

S
St Albans, Duke of .. 42
St Birinus 15
St Ives Hotel 79
St Ives Road 79
St Joseph's Church .. 74
St Luke's Church .. 34
St Mark's Church .. 79
St Mark's Hospital .. 79
St Peter's Church .. 73
Salmon 64
Salter's Fleet 65
Salvation Army .. 34, 42
Saxons 13, 14
Schools 127
Schwab, Hugo 34
Sedition 125
Shallop 65
Shaw, G. B. 67
Shoppenhanger Road .. 13
Shoppenhangers Manor 23
Shottesbrooke College of
St John 23
Shottesbrooke, Manor of 21, 77
Showboat, The .. 59, 112
Shrewsbury, Earl of .. 29
Silver, Richard .. 14, 90, 93
Simkin, Mrs, pink .. 94
Skindles 60, 89
Skindles, William .. 66
Smith, John .. 22, 112
Smith, W. H. & Sons .. 91
Smoking 42
Society of Friends .. 33
Soup kitchen 60
South Ellington .. 21
Special constables .. 126
Spencer, Manor of .. 21
Spencer, Sir Stanley RA 77
Spencer's Farm 112
Spindler's 92
Standford Univ. .. 79
Steam laundry 94
Steamers, Salter's .. 66
Stone masons 90
Stone Age implements .. 13
Stubbings House .. 59
Stuchbery & Thompson.. 93
Stuchbery, James .. 90
Stuchbery, Owen .. 93
Stuchbery, Mrs Owen .. 92
Stuchbery, Richard .. 93
Stuchbery, Thomas .. 90
Stuchbery, Thos. Wm. .. 93
Stuchbery, William .. 93
Sub rosa 30
Such, Clara 94
Such, Frdk. P. .. 89, 94
Summer Cloud 93
Sunny's Club 112
Susa's Band 91
Sutherland, Duchess of .. 67
Swan Upping 68
Swimming Pool 91
Swords, iron 14
Sydney, Earl of .. 29

T
Taeppa 14
Taplow Court 21, 60, 66, 78
Taplow Court parties .. 67
"Taplow Court", loco .. 78
Taylor, Joseph 40
Taylor, Robt. 40
Thames Acts 63
Thames Conservancy .. 63
Thames Cup 111
Thames Dammed .. 13
Thames Walk Scheme .. 64
Thicket 14
Thompson, Jane.. 92, 93
Thompson, Phil... .. 89
Thompson, S. R. .. 93
Thurber, James 112
Timberlake, H. K. 94, 112
Tithingmen 126
Tittle Row 14
Tollgates 42
Town Centre plan .. 139
Town Hall .. 22, 128
Traders (1760) 90
Trades 40
Tramps 41, 126
Trout 64, 65
Turk, John 68
Twin Towns 140
Twyford 14

U
Upson, Arthur 34
Upson, Dorothy 34

V
Vandervell, Tony .. 113
Vansittart, Colonel .. 125
Vanwall Special .. 113
Verderer, Windsor Forest 23
Victoria, Queen 67
Villa, Roman 14
Villiers, George 79
Vooght, E. Norman .. 59

W
Waldron, Mr G. L. .. 68
Wales, Charles, Prince of 139
Walker, Fdk. 77
Wallace, Edgar 111
Waltham Abbey 22
Waltham St Lawrence .. 22
War, civil 29
War Graves Commission 140
Warden, first 40
Warfield 22
Warwick the Kingmaker 23
Water Co 91
Waterside Inn 67
Webber, H. S. 78
Webber, J. C. 91
Wesleyan Church .. 33
West London Aero Club 60
West Saxons 14
Weyer, William Van de. 77
White Hart Inn .. 91, 92
White Horse Inn .. 40
White Waltham 14
Whitfield, Richard .. 22
Wilberforce, Wm. .. 22
Wilder family 65
Wilhelmina, Queen .. 59
William & Mary .. 30
William, the Conqueror.. 15
Windsor, Duke of .. 111
Windsor Forest .. 23
Winter Hill 42
Wireless 93
W.V.S. 59

Y
Yellow Ribbon Army .. 42
York Road Chapel .. 33

ENDPAPERS: 1974 Aerial photographs.